A World of
Poetry
Third Edition

Edited by
Mark McWatt
Hazel Simmons-McDonald

HODDER
EDUCATION
AN HACHETTE UK COMPANY

Hachette UK's policy is to use papers that are natural, renewable and recyclable products and made from wood grown in sustainable forests. The logging and manufacturing processes are expected to conform to the environmental regulations of the country of origin.

Orders: please contact Bookpoint Ltd, 130 Park Drive, Milton Park, Abingdon, Oxon OX14 4SE. Telephone: (44) 01235 827720. Fax: (44) 01235 400454. Email: education@bookpoint.co.uk Lines are open from 9 a.m. to 5 p.m., Monday to Saturday, with a 24-hour message answering service. You can also order through our website: www.hoddereducation.com

ISBN 9781510414310

© Hodder & Stoughton Ltd 2017

The CXC logo® and CSEC® are registered trademarks of the Caribbean Examinations Council (CXC)

First edition published 1994
Second edition published 2005 by Pearson Education Ltd, published from 2015 by Hodder Education
This edition published 2017 by Hodder Education

An Hachette UK Company
Carmelite House
50 Victoria Embankment
London EC4Y 0DZ
www.hoddereducation.com

Impression number   10 9 8 7 6 5 4 3 2 1

Year   2021 2020 2019 2018 2017

Typeset by Integra Software Services Pvt. Ltd., Pondicherry, India

Cover illustration by Mehrdokht Amini

Printed and bound in the UK

A catalogue record for this title is available from the British Library.

Contents

Contents

PEOPLE AND DESIRES

PEOPLE   65

FROM TIME TO ETERNITY

ART, ARTIST, ARTEFACT   **166**

NOSTALGIA   **175**

DEATH   **185**

> The following icon is used in this book:
>
> **p.000** This indicates the page number of the notes and questions which accompany the poem or vice versa.

Introduction

Dear students and teachers,

For this third edition of *A World of Poetry*, we have removed 76 of the 139 poems that were in the second edition and replaced them with 93 new poems. There are now 156 poems in the book, with the extra ones perhaps reflecting a slightly greater emphasis on the work of contemporary Caribbean poets.

While we have kept the book's organisation into twelve sections, each reflecting the dominant theme of the poems, we do not intend this organisation to dictate the order in which you read them. You will discover that several of the poems explore more than one theme and may fit just as well into a different section. Teachers, you may wish to choose two (or more) poems from any of the thematic groups and devise questions that help your students to read the poems carefully, while focusing their attention on the broader themes.

As you are probably aware, CXC specifically tests a candidate's ability to compare and synthesise information from two or more sources. To develop this skill, you can devise questions on two poems having the same theme or even on individual poems, particularly longer ones, that will focus on the way(s) in which their different parts relate to each other and to the central idea or theme.

You may find the notes and questions at the end of each section useful for initiating discussion on individual poems. Our questions are not exhaustive, and they do not focus on every aspect of the poems deserving comment. Students, we think it is important for you to interpret, analyse and explore the deeper levels of meaning in the poems, and that too long a list of questions might restrict your discussions and limit the process of discovery.

We have also included general information on poetic genre and form, and notes on figurative language. We hope that these will help you to recognise poetic devices when you encounter them in your reading, and that you will be better able to understand why they are used and how they contribute to the overall richness and meaning of individual poems.

While we have chosen several poems that we think a CXC candidate should study, we have also tried to include poems that will appeal to your interests. We hope that you will experience delight and intellectual stimulation from reading the poems in this book.

Mark McWatt and Hazel Simmons-McDonald

THE CHILD AND THE WORLD

NATURE

Childhood of a Voice

The light oppresses and the darkness frees
a man like me, who never cared at all:
Imagine it, the childhood of a voice
and voice of childhood telling me my name.

5   But if only the rain would fall,
and the sky we have not seen so long
come blue again.

The familiar white street
is tired of always running east.
10   The sky, of always arching over.
The tree, of always reaching up.

Even the round earth is tired of being round
and spinning round the sun.

Martin Carter

p.17

A Lesson for this Sunday

The growing idleness of summer grass
With its frail kites of furious butterflies
Requests the lemonade of simple praise
In scansion gentler than my hammock swings
5   And rituals no more upsetting than a
Black maid shaking linen as she sings
The plain notes of some protestant hosanna
Since I lie idling from the thought in things,

Or so they should. Until I hear the cries
10   Of two small children hunting yellow wings,
Who break my sabbath with the thought of sin.

Brother and sister, with a common pin,
Frowning like serious lepidopterists.
The little surgeon pierces the thin eyes.

15 Crouched on plump haunches, as a mantis prays
She shrieks to eviscerate its abdomen.
The lesson is the same. The maid removes
Both prodigies from their interest in science.
The girl, in lemon frock, begins to scream

20 As the maimed, teetering thing attempts its flight.
She is herself a thing of summery light.
Frail as a flower in this blue August air,
Not marked for some late grief that cannot speak.

The mind swings inward on itself in fear
25 Swayed towards nausea from each normal sign.
Heredity of cruelty everywhere,
And everywhere the frocks of summer torn,
The long look back to see where choice is born,
As summer grass sways to the scythe's design.

p.17 *Derek Walcott*

Hurt Hawks

I
The broken pillar of the wing jags from the clotted shoulder,
The wing trails like a banner in defeat,

No more to use the sky forever but live with famine
And pain a few days: cat nor coyote
5 Will shorten the week of waiting for death, there is game without talons.

He stands under the oak-bush and waits
The lame feet of salvation; at night he remembers freedom
And flies in a dream, the dawns ruin it.

He is strong and pain is worse to the strong, incapacity is worse.

10 The curs of the day come and torment him
At distance, no one but death the redeemer will humble that head,

The intrepid readiness, the terrible eyes.
The wild God of the world is sometimes merciful to those
That ask mercy, not often to the arrogant.

15 You do not know him, you communal people, or you have forgotten him;
Intemperate and savage, the hawk remembers him;
Beautiful and wild, the hawks, and men that are dying, remember him.

II
I'd sooner, except the penalties, kill a man than a hawk;
but the great redtail
20 Had nothing left but unable misery
From the bone too shattered for mending, the wing that trailed under his talons
    when he moved.

We had fed him six weeks, I gave him freedom,
He wandered over the foreland hill and returned in the evening, asking for death,
Not like a beggar, still eyed with the old
25 Implacable arrogance.

I gave him the lead gift in the twilight.
What fell was relaxed, Owl-downy, soft feminine feathers; but what
Soared: the fierce rush: the night-herons by the flooded river cried fear at its rising
Before it was quite unsheathed from reality.

p.17 *Robinson Jeffers*

Birdshooting Season

Birdshooting season the men
make marriages with their guns
My father's house turns macho
as from far the hunters gather

5   All night long contentless women
stir their brews: hot coffee
chocolata, cerassie
wrap pone and tie-leaf
for tomorrow's sport. Tonight
10   the men drink white rum neat.

In darkness shouldering
their packs, their guns, they leave

We stand quietly on the
doorstep shivering. Little boys
15   longing to grow up birdhunters too
Little girls whispering:
Fly Birds Fly.

p.18

Olive Senior

Hedgehog

The snail moves like a
Hovercraft, held up by a
Rubber cushion of itself,
Sharing its secret

5   With the hedgehog. The hedgehog
Shares its secret with no one.
We say, Hedgehog, come out
Of yourself and we will love you.

We mean no harm. We want
10   Only to listen to what
You have to say. We want
Your answers to our questions.

The hedgehog gives nothing
Away, keeping itself to itself.
15 We wonder what a hedgehog
Has to hide, why it so distrusts.

We forget the god
Under this crown of thorns.
We forget that never again
20 Will a god trust in the world.
p.18 *Paul Muldoon*

Schooldays

Every nun wears a ring
– Brides of God.
An astonishing act,
as if depictions of hell
5 came true with brush-marks
and artists cheering.

Rain is wetting windows,
but what about trees
witnessing the Bride of God
10 deprive little boys of sin.

For each nun, God and boy,
strings of colour
and separate balconies
link all realities as
15 another astonishing act.
But the sunset is yours,
the garden of guavas mine,
and God can have the rest.
p.18 *Stanley Greaves*

An African Thunderstorm

From the west
Clouds come hurrying with the wind
Turning
Sharply
5   Here and there
Like a plague of locusts
Whirling
Tossing up things on its tail
Like a madman chasing nothing.
10   Pregnant clouds
Ride stately on its back
Gathering to perch on hills
Like dark sinister wings;
The Wind whistles by
15   And trees bend to let it pass.

In the village
Screams of delighted children
Toss and turn
In the din of the whirling wind.
20   Women –
Babies clinging on their backs –
Dart about
In and out
Madly
25   The Wind whirls by
Whilst trees bend to let it pass.
Clothes wave like tattered flags
Flying off
To expose dangling breasts
30   As jaggered blinding flashes

Rumble, tremble, and crack
Amidst the smell of fired smoke
And the pelting march of the storm.

p.18
David Rubadiri

Those Winter Sundays

Sundays too my father got up early
and put his clothes on in the blueblack cold,
then with cracked hands that ached
from labor in the weekday weather made
5   banked fires blaze. No one ever thanked him.

I'd wake and hear the cold splintering, breaking.
When the rooms were warm, he'd call,
and slowly I would rise and dress,
fearing the chronic angers of that house,

10   Speaking indifferently to him,
who had driven out the cold
and polished my good shoes as well.
What did I know, what did I know
of love's austere and lonely offices?

p.19
Robert Hayden

A Quartet of Daffodils

I think it must be spring
because yesterday morning on Spadina
there was an Indian woman walking
wrapped in maximum eight yards of sari cloth.
5   It was sheer and a luminous color
like the nectar of pressed apricots.

A red dot punctuated the center of her brow,
like a small and urgent point of energy
had found its way to the surface of her skin,
10 and jeweled or a drop of blood, it was gleaming.
I think it must be spring because
there is not a host but a quartet of daffodils

sprung up in the front yard of Gore Vale.
They stand not straight but bowed over so.
15 I think that they had a hard time making it out
of their frozen birthplace inside the earth.
Nevertheless, they are here and have come in first.
The runners-up are the crocuses.

But the evergreen never went under,
20 it just spread its branches taut and took the worst
that winter had to offer. Do not go under
and one day you may be crowned with evergreen.
This year is my third spring, the third time
that I have been witness to the cycle of the seasons.

25 Where I am born, there is no such thing,
seasons just shift over a bit to accommodate
the one following. Our winters bring tangerines
and pimento winds. Bless now death, resurrection,
the peculiar ascension of ice falls finally away.

30 I think it must be spring now because today
I feel so tender, like all early things budding.
And even if I am coming in exhausted,
bowed, bent, drawn, and yellow-skinned
like my very first quartet of daffodils
35 I know now that this is undeniably spring.

p.19   *Lorna Goodison*

Landscape Painter

(*For Albert Huie*)

I watch him set up easel,
Both straddling precariously
A corner of the twisted, climbing
Mountain track

5   A tireless humming-bird, his brush
Dips, darts, hovers now here, now there,
Where puddles of pigment
Bloom in the palette's wild small garden.

The mountains pose for him
10   In a family group
Dignified, self-conscious, against the wide blue screen
Of morning; low green foot-hills
Sprawl like grandchildren about the knees
Of seated elders. And behind them, aloof,
15   Shouldering the sky, patriarchal in serenity,
Blue Mountain Peak bulks.

And the professional gaze
Studies positions, impatiently waiting
For the perfect moment to fix
20   Their preparedness, to confine them
For the pleasant formality
Of the family album.

His brush a humming-bird
Meticulously poised …
25   The little hills fidgeting,
Changelessly changing,
Artlessly frustrating
The painter's art.

p.19   *Vivian Virtue*

Janet Waking

Beautifully Janet slept
Till it was deeply morning. She woke then
And thought about her dainty-feathered hen,
To see how it had kept.

5   One kiss she gave her mother.
One a small one gave she to her daddy
Who would have kissed each curl of his shining baby
No kiss at all for her brother.

'Old Chucky, old Chucky!' she cried.
10   Running across the world upon the grass
To Chucky's house, and listening. But alas,
Her Chucky had died.

It was a transmogrifying bee
Came droning down on Chucky's old bald head
15   And sat and put the poison. It scarcely bled,
But how exceedingly

And purply did the knot
Swell with the venom and communicate
Its rigor! Now the poor comb stood up straight
20   But Chucky did not.

So there was Janet
Kneeling on the wet grass, crying her brown hen
(Translated far beyond the daughters of men)
To rise and walk upon it.

25   And weeping fast as she had breath
Janet implored us, 'Wake her from her sleep!'
And would not be instructed in how deep
Was the forgetful kingdom of death.

John Crowe Ransom

p.19

Their Lonely Betters

As I listened from a beach-chair in the shade
To all the noises that my garden made,
It seemed to me only proper that words
Should be withheld from vegetables and birds

5   A robin with no Christian name ran through
The Robin-Anthem which was all it knew,
And rustling flowers for some third party waited
To say which pairs, if any, should get mated.

Not one of them was capable of lying,
10   There was not one which knew that it was dying
Or could have with a rhythm or a rhyme
Assumed responsibility for time.

Let them leave language to their lonely betters
Who count some days and long for certain letters;
15   We, too, make noises when we laugh or weep:
Words are for those with promises to keep.

p.20

W.H. Auden

Responsibility

I half awaken
to the comforting blur of my mother
pulling on her house-
dress in the half dark

5   and already the sound of my father
as from muted dream distance
clucking the chickens to corn.

I too some distant morning
shall rise responsibly
10   to set my house in motion.

Meantime, I pull the covers close
and smile for the pure secret
thrill of it, and ease myself down
into that last, sweet, morning sleep.
Edward Baugh

p.20

Dove Song

'Yuh hear dem doves? Somebody gwine home
To dey Maker soon.' (Granny)

I do not like this mourning
of the dove,
that darkens dawn
and mocks at love.
5   I like the quickness
of the sparrow's chirp,
the brisk blackbird's song.

I do not like
this contrapuntal error,
10   a cleft, in the mind's peace;
a slowing of the heart
against the will,
against light on lime trees,
the brightness of the red hibiscus.

15   This persistence of discord,
a swelling sadness,
too close
not far away.

20 This dove mourning
broken olive branches,
forsaken ark.
This dove mourning,
calling, calling …

p.20 *Esther Phillips*

Ground Doves

Small querulous birds
feathers like swatches of earth
graced with wings,
opt for walking.

5 The female ones
sport surprising underslips
trimmed with stunning passementerie.
Braided arabesques

scalloping round their hems
10 but that is rarely shown, except
when they bend to scramble
for stale bread crumbs

they have come to expect as due.
Ground doves make you uneasy
15 because there was a time
when you too walked

and saved your wings
and would not reach high
for the sweet risk
20 inside the lips of hibiscus

but saved your wings,
and scrambled for used bread
and left over things …

p.20 *Lorna Goodison*

Horses

All the pink-coloured horses are coming in.
They gallop in from the sunset, hearts
beating like a drum.

Unbridled, they canter,
5   Flushed. Approaching twilight.
Behind, Sun is a blaze of metal
Sinking into the sea.

Where are the golden horsemen?
They too are drowning.
10   They will rise from the sea tomorrow.
Their dust will rise up from the east.

Meanwhile, the horses come in,
last troops in the twilight,
with their hoofs of steel, their wild manes.
15   The drums from the Amazon are thundering and
breasty women are blowing into the fire.

The children are petulant, sucking their thumbs
with outcast expressions.
It is suppertime and their stomachs are groaning.

20   But outside the hut, the men
are hammering the goatskin drums with their fingers.
They wait for the horses to come in.

p.21 *Mahadai Das*

Keep off the Grass

The grass is a green mat
trimmed with gladioli
red like flames in a furnace.
The park bench, hallowed,
5   holds the loiterer listening
to the chant of the fountain
showering holy water on a congregation
of pigeons.

Then madam walks her Pekinese,
10   bathed and powdered and perfumed.
He sniffs at the face of the 'Keep off' sign
with a nose as cold as frozen fish
and salutes it with a hind paw
leaving it weeping in anger and shame.

p.21   *Oswald Mbuyiseni Mtshali*

Notes and questions

Some of the poems in this section describe the simple beauty of nature while others focus on wildlife and the hunting of animals. Other selections are about pets and some explore the effect of the loss of a pet on its owner. Other poems deal with experiences at school. The power of the elements and death as an inevitable natural occurrence are other themes reflected here.

Childhood of a Voice

- What is the persona of this poem longing for?

- How would you describe the mood of the speaker of the poem?

- How do the last six lines of the poem (lines 8–13) emphasise this mood?

- Discuss the title of the poem with your classmates. How appropriate is it for the subject matter that the poem deals with?

A Lesson for this Sunday

'lepidopterists' (line 13) – people who study and/or collect moths/butterflies.

'heredity' (line 26) – transmission of genetic factors (that determine individual characteristics) from one generation to another.

- What is the poet doing in the first stanza and what is he musing about?

- What were the children doing in stanza 2 that disturbed the poet?

- What is the point of the poet's statement about the girl in the last three lines of stanza 2?

- What do you think 'Heredity of cruelty everywhere' (line 26) means in the context of the last stanza and the rest of the poem? Explain the lesson referred to in the title of the poem.

Hurt Hawks

- Why is death inevitable for the hawk?

- Why won't 'cat nor coyote' (line 4) put the hawk out if its misery?

- What do stanzas 4 and 5 tell us about the 'character' of the wounded hawk?

- Explain in your own words what happens in the final stanza.

p.4

Birdshooting Season

- Explain what is meant by 'the men/make marriages with their guns' (lines 1–2).

- Why are the women described as 'contentless' (line 5)?

- Explain the difference in the attitudes between the males and females towards the hunting season.

 p.5

Hedgehog

'Hovercraft' (line 2) – a vehicle that moves over land or water, supported by a cushion of air generated by downward-directed fans.

- What is the 'secret' shared between a snail and a hedgehog? What are the similarities between them?

- Explain why it is difficult to love a hedgehog.

- How does the final stanza take the poem to another level of meaning?

 p.6

Schooldays

- What is the 'astonishing act' referred to in line 3 of the poem?

- The persona expresses scepticism in the first stanza. What is he sceptical about?

- Explain in your own words exactly what the trees witness (lines 8–9).

- What do you think is the 'sin' referred to in line 10?

- The images in the last stanza are presented as in a painting. Pick out these images and explain what the 'astonishing act' is in line 15.

- What point is the poet stressing in the assertions made in the last three lines of the poem?

 p.7

An African Thunderstorm

- The poet uses several different images to describe the gathering storm. Focus on these images and discuss the specific effects the poet creates with each one.

- What is the effect of the repetition of 'The Wind .../... trees bend to let it pass' at the end of stanza 1 (lines 14–15) and in stanza 2 (lines 25–26)?

- Look carefully at the diction (the choice of words and phrases). What is particularly striking about it?

Those Winter Sundays

'indifferently' (line 10) – showing no care, concern or interest.

- Consider the things that the father does. What do they suggest about him?

- What was the son's attitude towards the father when he was a child? How has it changed?

- What do you think are the 'chronic angers' (line 9) of the house?

- Explain the last two lines of the poem.

A Quartet of Daffodils

'Spadina' (line 2) – a major north–south street in the west of downtown Toronto.

'… not a host but a quartet of daffodils' (line 12) – this is a reference to a well-known poem by Wordsworth, 'I Wandered Lonely as a Cloud', in which he refers to 'a crowd, a host of golden daffodils'.

- Explain the last two lines of stanza 3.

- Why is spring a relatively new experience for the poet?

- What does stanza 5 tell us about the poet's home country?

Landscape Painter

- In this poem, a metaphor of a family posing for a portrait is used to present the landscape. How is this sustained throughout the poem? Find the lines in the poem that capture the family image.

- 'For the perfect moment to fix/Their preparedness, to confine them' (lines 19–20). To what do you think these lines refer? What is the 'perfect moment'?

- In what ways is the painter's brush like a 'humming-bird' (line 23)?

- Discuss how stanza 4 helps both to clarify and extend the central metaphor used in the poem.

Janet Waking

'transmogrify' (line 13) – to change or transform into a different shape, especially a bizarre or grotesque one.

- What point is being emphasised, do you think, by the description of Janet's way of greeting her family (stanza 2) and her response to the hen (stanzas 3, 6 and 7)?

- Explain what happened to the hen.

- Discuss with your classmates the appropriateness and significance of the title of the poem.

Their Lonely Betters

- What is this poem saying about the plants and creatures of nature?

- What are the shortcomings and limitations of natural things, as described in stanza 3?

- Who or what are the 'lonely betters' (line 13) described in stanza 4? Explain why 'lonely' and why 'better'.

Responsibility

- What, in the view of the persona of the poem, are the things that represent responsibility?

- With what are these things contrasted?

- Consider the use of the phrases 'comforting blur' (line 2) and 'muted dream distance' (line 6), and comment on their contribution to the meaning of the poem.

Dove Song

- In what ways is the dove contrasted with the sparrow and the blackbird in lines 5–7?

- The mourning of the dove is described as a 'contrapuntal error' (line 9). What does this phrase and the lines which follow (lines 10–23) emphasise about the call of the dove?

- What do the allusions to 'broken olive branches' (line 20) and 'forsaken ark' (line 21) bring to mind?

- What effect is created by the persona's repetition of 'I do not like' at the beginning of stanzas 1 and 2?

Ground Doves

'passementerie' (line 7) – a trimming of gold or silver lace, or braids or beads.

'arabesques' (line 8) – a term used in ballet to describe a posture; (also refers to) a design of intertwined leaves or scrolls.

- The ground doves evoke different feelings in the persona. What are these feelings? What is it about the doves that evokes these feelings?

- How do the last two stanzas explain the persona's discomfort about the walking of the doves?

Horses

- To what do the 'pink-coloured horses' in line 1 refer? Why are they described as pink? What do you think are their 'hearts' that make a sound 'like a drum' (lines 2–3)?

- Reference is made in stanza 3 to 'golden horsemen' (line 8). Who or what do you think they are?

- In what ways do the last three stanzas present a contrast to the first three?

Keep off the Grass

- What do you think is the purpose of the careful description of the scene in stanza 1 and of the Pekinese in stanza 2?

- What does 'with a nose as cold as frozen fish/and salutes it with a hind paw' (lines 12–13) suggest about the dog's attitude?

- What attributes are given to the 'Keep off' sign?

- Explain the meaning of the last line of the poem.

CHILDHOOD EXPERIENCES

My Parents

My parents kept me from children who were rough
Who threw words like stones and who wore torn clothes.
Their thighs showed through rags. They ran in the street
And climbed cliffs and stripped by the country streams.

5   I feared more than tigers their muscles like iron
Their jerking hands and their knees tight on my arms.
I feared the salt coarse pointing of those boys
Who copied my lisp behind me on the road.

They were lithe, they sprang out behind hedges
10   Like dogs to bark at my world. They threw mud
While I looked the other way, pretending to smile.
I longed to forgive them, but they never smiled.

Stephen Spender

Journal

(*For Melanie*)

My daughter, bent
like a sapling
in the wind of her imagination
has cast off on an ocean
5   where I flounder
with each page
that washes by.
When she was born
I learned the swimmer's truth:
10   you drown if you can dream
of drowning, if you learn
to read too well.

I turned to treading water
then, narrowing
15   my eyes against
the salt of metaphor,
the dazzle of the sunlight
on the seas' bright margins.

I feared the white roar
20   underneath the silence
of the sun-struck afternoons.

Time, like an ocean, makes us
islands all. The sea-gulls
shriek across the arid green
25   of waves eroding every coast,
each half-moon of a beach
that limits every village
to an alphabet
of necessary gesture.

30   I built her paper boats
when she was three
out of discarded poems
and the letters I could never send to my father.

Now I wake up to lavender,
35   the sky above the blue ridge
bruised with light, the grey chill
edged with woodsmoke. Sometimes
she voyages all night, chained
to the mast of some unwieldy narrative.
40   I free her into sleep
at fore-day morning, then
I trudge down to the waiting water,
hoping to drown again.

p.44   *David Williams*

A Song in the Front Yard

I've stayed in the front yard all my life.
I want to peek at the back
Where it's rough and untended and hungry weed grows.
A girl gets sick of a rose.

5   I want to go in the back yard now
And maybe down the alley,
To where the charity children play.
I want a good time today.

They do some wonderful things.
10   They have some wonderful fun.
My mother sneers, but I say it's fine
How they don't have to go in at quarter to nine.
My mother, she tells me that Johnnie Mae
Will grow up to be a bad woman.
15   That George'll be taken to Jail soon or late
(On account of last winter he sold our back gate).

But I say it's fine. Honest, I do.
And I'd like to be a bad woman, too,
And wear the brave stockings of night-black lace
20   And strut down the streets with paint on my face.

Gwendolyn Brooks

p.44

Fern Hill

Now as I was young and easy under the apple boughs
About the lilting house and happy as the grass was green,
     The night above the dingle starry,
       Time let me hail and climb
5   Golden in the heydays of his eyes,
And honoured among wagons I was prince of the apple towns

And once below a time I lordly had the trees and leaves
        Trail with daisies and barley
      Down the rivers of the windfall light.

10   And as I was green and carefree, famous among the barns
About the happy yard and singing as the farm was home,
       In the sun that is young once only,
         Time let me play and be
       Golden in the mercy of his means,
15   And green and golden I was huntsman and herdsman, the calves
Sang to my horn, the foxes on the hills barked clear and cold,
        And the sabbath rang slowly
      In the pebbles of the holy streams.

All the sun long it was running, it was lovely, the hay
20   Fields high as the house, the tunes from the chimneys, it was air
       And playing, lovely and watery
        And fire green as grass.
       And nightly under the simple stars
As I rode to sleep the owls were bearing the farm away,
25   All the moon long I heard, blessed among stables, the night-jars
       Flying with the ricks, and the horses
        Flashing into the dark.

And then to awake, and the farm, like a wanderer white
With the dew, come back, the cock on his shoulder: it was all
30   Shining, it was Adam and maiden,
        The sky gathered again
       And the sun grew round that very day.
So it must have been after the birth of the simple light
In the first, spinning place, the spellbound horses walking warm
35   Out of the whinnying green stable
         On to the fields of praise.

And honoured among foxes and pheasants by the gay house
Under the new made clouds and happy as the heart was long,
    In the sun born over and over,
40   I ran my heedless ways,
    My wishes raced through the house high hay
And nothing I cared, at my sky blue trades, that time allows
In all his tuneful turning so few and such morning songs
    Before the children green and golden
45   Follow him out of grace.

Nothing I cared, in the lamb white days, that time would take me
Up to the swallow thronged loft by the shadow of my hand,
    In the moon that is always rising,
      Nor that riding to sleep
50   I should hear him fly with the high fields
And wake to the farm forever fled from the childless land.
Oh as I was young and easy in the mercy of his means,
    Time held me green and dying
    Though I sang in my chains like the sea.

p.45   *Dylan Thomas*

Counter

He was in prison,
his brother called to say.
I learned he was considered counter

to the ideas of the revolution,
5   that he planned with a counter group.
He was in prison.

I used to be his teacher, I explained.
He's young, I said, foolish perhaps, not dangerous.
I learned he was considered counter.

10 I saw his calm face in the second row
    and knew I was too close to that distress.
    He was in prison.

    Months later, he was released, no charge.
    I saw his listening face in the second row.
15 I learned he was considered counter.
    Artist, teacher, vacillator, I found no counter answer.
    Merle Collins

p.45

Overseer: Detention

    The afternoons grew more humid
    on Thursdays when there was detention,
    boys gathered in a room, unsettlingly quiet,
    half-asleep, making jets with homework
5   papers – the teacher as bored as the students.
    Sometimes, the Boss hosted 'repeat offenders'
    in a Detention Special, and we lined up
    with rags, gloves and rubbing-alcohol,
    were marshalled about the school, rubbing
10 out our cannon of graffiti, bursting out laughing
    when we came across drawings
    of penises, our mothers' breasts or the
    one heroic epigram saying, 'Boss, bullar'.
    We sprayed and wiped off our names, losing
15 ourselves in the fumes of the alcohol.
    Boss carried a half-smile the whole
    time. You could always catch him
    doing this – smiling from somewhere deep
    inside him, as if from knowing that
20 every crop of boys will find a way
    to disturb the walls of his authority,
    and he will punish them like budding Mau Mau,

nèg mawon. He wanted to be here
for all of it, all the repeating shapes
25   of that lifelong game, where the more things changed
was the more they stayed the same.

Vladimir Lucien

English Girl Eats Her First Mango

If I did tell she
hold this gold
of sundizzy
tonguelicking juicy
5   mouthwater flow
ripe with love
from the tropics

she woulda tell me
trust you to be
10   mellowdramatic

so I just say
taste this mango

and I watch she hold
the smooth cheeks
15   of the mango
blushing yellow
and a glow
rush to she own cheeks

and she ask me
20   what do I do now
just bite into it?

and I was tempted
to tell she

25 why not be a devil
and eat of the skin
of original sin

but she woulda tell me
trust you to be
mysterious

30 so I just say
it's up to you
if you want to peel it

and I watch she feel it
as something precious
35 then she smile and say
looks delicious

and I tell she
don't waste sweet words

when sweetness
40 in your hand

just bite it man
peel it with the teeth
that God gave you

or better yet
45 do like me mother
used to do

and squeeze
till the flesh
turn syrup
50 nibble a hole
then suck the gold
like bubby
in child mouth

squeeze and tease out
55   every drop of spice

sounds nice
me friend tell me

and I remind she
that this ain't
60   apple core
so don't forget
the seed
suck that too
the sweetest part
65   the juice does run
down to your heart

man if you see
the English rose
she face was bliss
70   down to the pink
of she toes

and when she finish
she smile
and turn to me

75   lend me your hanky
my fingers
are all sticky
with mango juice

and I had to tell she
80   what hanky
you talking bout

you don't know
when you eat mango

85 you hanky
    is your tongue

    man just lick
    you finger
    you call that
    culture
90 lick you finger
    you call that
    culture

    unless you prefer
    to call it
95 colonisation
    in reverse

p.46 *John Agard*

Walking on Lily Leaves

The brown boys have a game they play: it is a rare
    philosophical game.
In the streams under the old trees when they slow to
    sluggish ponds,
5 where stick-bodied dragonflies with red paper wings are
    adroit in skips on the surface,
water lilies grow from the stones and their green leaves
    float on the water.
Fully grown the leaves are almost tough enough to stand in
10   but not quite.
So each boy will jump softly from the bank full of ferns
    to one leaf, a second
before it sinks jump to another leaf as deftly as tallymen
    and the game ends at the end of water lilies.
15 The floating leaves are of course crushed into the sluggish
    water and the lily flowers go too.

I played that game. I hear still the laughter on the
    lady-slippered bank.
Death in the long river of lilies invades my heart,

20
p.46
    grown old, grown iron.
Ian McDonald

Little Boy Crying

Your mouth contorting in brief spite and hurt,
your laughter metamorphosed into howls,
your frame so recently relaxed now tight
with three-year-old frustration, your bright eyes

5   swimming tears, splashing your bare feet,
you stand there angling for a moment's hint
of guilt or sorrow for the quick slap struck.

The ogre towers above you, that grim giant,
empty of feeling, a colossal cruel,

10   soon victim of the tale's conclusion, dead
at last. You hate him, you imagine
chopping clean the tree he's scrambling down
or plotting deeper pits to trap him in.

You cannot understand, not yet,

15   the hurt your easy tears can scald him with,
nor guess the wavering hidden behind that mask.
This fierce man longs to lift you, curb your sadness
with piggy-back or bull-fight, anything,
but dare not ruin the lessons you should learn.

20
p.46
You must not make a plaything of the rain.
Mervyn Morris

School Play

(For Pat Allan)

My son's in love with
Cinderella's more wicked sister.
She has up-staged Cinderella
and spitting spite, hissing hate
5   struts her stuff downstage centre
while he stands with the chorus
mesmerized by her mascara eyes
flashing ten-year-old fury.

Cinderella, spark of the class,
10   has, in his eyes, been banished
to her rightful place among the cinders.
She has not fire enough
to flame his boyish fancy.

For all he cares, she can win
15   forty thousand princes.
The bewildered boy just knows
that all their love for this good girl
can't match the sum of his affection
for the artful sibling.

20   I, spectator to this drama,
applaud with glee to see her fall.
Her sudden change to goodness
can't erase a certain feeling
that she just won't do.

25   But how to warn him, yet so young,
deceived, as all men are, by outward seemliness?
Though now all fun, all art,

I know that someday, he'll arrive with one.
Then I'll applaud and smile as at a play –
30   the best performance of my life.
Hazel Simmons-McDonald

The Child Ran Into the Sea

The child ran into the sea
but ran back from the waves, because
the child did not know the sea
on the horizon, is not the same sea
5   ravishing the shore.

What every child wants is always
in the distance; like the sea
on the horizon. While, on the shore
nearby, at the feet of every child
10   shallow water, eating the edges
of islands and continents does little more,
little more than foam like spittle
at the corners of the inarticulate mouth
of some other child who wants to run
15   into the sea, into the horizon.
Martin Carter

Wharf Story

Once upon a time, and not so long ago,
I saw Bajan boys, fig-navalled, snotty-nosed,
gathering by the Bridgetown Wharf. Already rehearsed,

they wait in gaping shirts and pants,
5   shoeless and with knitted faces.
Foreign cameras, coins, and faces

advance towards the city. Rum-flushed, sun-burnt,
in rainbow shorts the visitors hurl pennies into the dark
current and await the water's howl.

10 They applaud (as boys bore like fantails
into the depths), and chatter like *Challenger's* crown
when two minutes pass. What if the experiment fails?

Soon, black hands puncture the surface; each raised trophy
acknowledged with a din. Jerked by that roar, a straw hat sails
15 into the murk. A fat man bellows: 'Boy, get my hat for me!'

The memory throbs with shame. Today, we are seduced
by a dawn that hymns a subtler story.
The conquistador slides inside our skin! He's reproduced

inside brick houses that mottle the heights and terraces,
20 a black man bellowing at his own, a black
child deaf to the strum of ancestral glory.

Anthony Kellman

Once Upon a Time

Once upon a time, son,
they used to laugh with their hearts
and laugh with their eyes;
but now they only laugh with their teeth,
5 while their ice-block-cold eyes
search behind my shadow.

There was a time indeed
they used to shake hands with their hearts;
but that's gone, son.
10 Now they shake hands without hearts
while their left hands search
my empty pockets.

'Feel at home!' 'Come again';
they say, and when I come
15 again and feel
at home, once, twice,
there will be no thrice –
for then I find doors shut on me.

So I have learned many things, son.
20 I have learned to wear many faces
like dresses – homeface,
officeface, streetface, hostface,
cocktailface, with all their conforming smiles
like a fixed portrait smile.

25 And I have learned, too,
to laugh with only my teeth
and shake hands without my heart.
I have also learned to say, 'Goodbye',
when I mean 'Good-riddance';
30 to say 'Glad to meet you',
without being glad; and to say 'It's been
nice talking to you', after being bored.

But believe me, son.
I want to be what I used to be
35 when I was like you. I want
to unlearn all these muting things.
Most of all, I want to relearn
how to laugh, for my laugh in the mirror
shows only my teeth like a snake's bare fangs!

40 So show me, son,
how to laugh; show me how
I used to laugh and smile
once upon a time when I was like you.

Gabriel Okara

p.47

How Dreams Grow Fat and Die

All summer I practised walking
in wooden-tip ballet shoes,
pretended God was pulling me up,
ten-year-old marionette,
5   steps stuttering from room to room.

Flat-footed I traced grout lines
in our kitchen with encyclopedias
on my head, balancing dreams of
twirling off stage into the sails
10   of standing ovations.

In September, you told my mother I
was too fat to be a ballerina.
You, of faux British accent and hollowed
collar bones I imagined were tea cups.

15   You, who wanted a *kukumkum* orchestra,
a herd of bones gliding under
the baton of your arms.

You, who illustrated to my mother
my incompetence by drawing a circle
20   in the air. I was the round nightmare
landing heavy in the melody of grand jetés.

You could keep me back with the younger
girls, maybe in a year or two I would shed
the fat, reverse blossom into fragrant bud,

25   or I could donate my tutu now
to the kingdom of dust cloths, hang my ballet
shoes by their wooden-tip necks.

In dreams I am a feather, buoyed and buoyant
and you are the barbed wire that kills me.

p.47

Tanya Shirley

Abra-Cadabra

My mother had more magic
in her thumb
than the length and breadth
of any magician

5   Weaving incredible stories
around the dark-green senna brew
just to make us slake
the ritual Sunday purgative

Knowing how to place a cochineal poultice
10   on a fevered forehead
Knowing how to measure a belly's symmetry
kneading the narah pains away

Once my baby sister stuffed
a split-pea up her nostril
15   my mother got a crochet needle
and gently tried to pry it out

We stood around her
like inquisitive gauldings

Suddenly, in surgeon's tone she ordered,
20   'Pass the black pepper,'
and patted a little
under the dozing nose

My baby sister sneezed.
The rest was history.

p.48

Grace Nichols

Aunt Jennifer's Tigers

Aunt Jennifer's tigers prance across a screen,
Bright topaz denizens of a world of green.
They do not fear the men beneath the tree;
They pace in sleek chivalric certainty.

5   Aunt Jennifer's fingers fluttering through her wool
Find even the ivory needle hard to pull.
The massive weight of Uncle's wedding band
Sits heavily upon Aunt Jennifer's hand.

When Aunt is dead, her terrified hands will lie
10   Still ringed with ordeals she was mastered by.
The tigers in the panel that she made
Will go on prancing, proud and unafraid.

Adrienne Rich

p.48

Kanaima/Tiger

(*For Richard and David*)

In the darkest middle of rubber walk
where the interweave of overhanging branches
was thick above the road, the four schoolboys
walking home (loitering in the roadside bush,
5   collecting shiny rubber seeds in their wooden pods)
suddenly stopped – movement, talk, breath,
all stopped: for there in the road, yards ahead,
stood a black tiger. He had appeared out of nowhere.
When I first saw him he was simply there; his cold
10   green eyes looked straight at us, four human statues
with shoulder-slung bookbags and gaping mouths.
He looked long, then turned his head and strode
into the bush on the other side of the road.

It was the first time any of us had seen

15   a black tiger. For the next two weeks they sent

the Land Rover to collect us after school,

making of the magical rubber walk

a ninety-second blur of dark green gloom

incensed with the damp smell of leaves. But

20   we were soon walking again, collecting rubber

seeds and daring each other to step

into the undergrowth and enter the darker

realm of the tiger. 'It wasn't a tiger,'

Jude Santiago had said, the day after we saw it;

25   'remember how he watch at we and think?

My father say tigers don't think. Was

Kanaima. Kanaima was looking for somebody:

lucky it wasn't we.' And he was right,

the creature did look at us and think.

30   So it was Kanaima … And yet something

in my head made Jude's dark certainty

impossible for me. My father was certain

it wasn't Kanaima; Jude was certain that it was,

and mine was that painful uncertainty

35   that helped define my childhood plight:

Caught between their 'wrong' and our 'right'.

Now time and distance have tamed the memory,

and the fear has drained away: I have

long since learned to say 'jaguar' instead of

40   'tiger' (in contexts where that kind of accuracy

matters). But whenever I rummage in the deepest

drawer of childhood memories, I still

cannot describe whether it was tiger or Kanaima

that looked hard as us that day, that

45   found us wanting and calmly walked away.

Mark McWatt

p.48

40

Jamaica Journal

He stands outside the fencing looking in.

Inside sunbathers relishing their flesh –
some white, some black, and some of other skins –
diving and swimming feign not to notice him,
5   fingers of doubt spread wide, gripping the holes of mesh.

Some people on the grass are picnicking.

His pants are torn; he does not have a shirt;
his face, a mask of sun-flaked grease and dirt
too young to understand his day's events,
10   dreams mountain-slide of magic dollars and cents
to cancel knowledge of the stomach's pain,
eyes learning what will later reach his brain.

In time they'll be afraid to hear his curse
at god's unholy sunday-school arrangement,
15   put him inside a wire mesh, or worse,
and sunbathe in the same sun on his hearse
or perish if his bullet gets them first.

 Cecil Gray

Comfort

I

They were the delight of dull afternoons, stretching in chants of multiplication
    tables.
They were comfort, wrapped in small squares of brown shop paper,
hidden in packed pockets, waiting to be sucked.
They were the ease of tedium,
5   Mr Sam made them. He timed our passing by his corner shop at a
quarter to eight each day.

II

We crowded the door, eager eyes follow his drama.
The shedding of stiffly starched shirt,
donning of vest, wrapping of apron round hips, washing and drying
10   of hands,
opening the window and wiping off yesterday's flakes from the nine-
inch nail driven into the lintel.

Next, his turning with studied grace to the kettle, sniffing to test the
strength of the mint.
15   Then, the moment that stilled our breaths;
his reaching into the pot to lift the cooled mint-flavoured mass in
practiced hands that held each drop.
His throwing it onto the nail, catching it in cupped hands.
Throwing again, first in a slow-mo dance of throw and catch,
20   throwing, catching, pulling,
whipping, the whole thing to whiteness till it hung a long pliant rope.

Then the reverent placing on the sugar-dusted counter top, the
whetting of knife, cutting of rope
into small pieces, and leaving them to harden before dropping them
25   into a large jar where
we would find them at lunch, on the counter top next to a pile of
small squares of brown paper
on which Mr Sam, now shirted, put two for a penny.

III

Now sometimes, when a day stretches before me in a tedious repetition
30   of marking squares of white paper,
I slip a rock-hard sweet in my mouth and recall the ritual of comfort-making.

p.49

Hazel Simmons-McDonald

Boy with Book of Knowledge

He holds a volume open in his hands;
Sepia portraits of the hairy great,
The presidents and poets in their beards
Alike, simplified histories of the wars,
5   Conundrums, quizzes, riddles, games and poems.

'Immortal Poems'; at least he can't forget them,
Barbara Frietchie and the Battle Hymn.
And best of all America the Beautiful,
Whose platitudinous splendors ended with
10   'From sea to shining sea,' and made him cry

And wish to be a poet, only to say such things,
From sea to shining sea. Could that have been
Where it began? The vast pudding of knowledge,
With poetry rare as raisins in the midst
15   Of those gold-lettered volumes black and green?

Mere piety to think so. But being now
As near his deathday as his birthday then,
He would acknowledge all he will not know,
The silent library brooding through the night
20   With all its lights continuing to burn

Insomniac, a luxury liner on what sea
Unfathomable of ignorance who could say?
And poetry, as steady, still and rare
As the lighthouses now unmanned and obsolete
25   That used to mark America's dangerous shores.

p.49

Howard Nemerov

Notes and questions

The poems in this section reveal that there are experiences which are common to childhood regardless of the culture in which one may grow up. Several of the poems explore responses to experiences like participating in childish escapades. Others focus on more serious themes like death, cruelty and confusion. Most of the poems are narrated from an adult perspective and are reflective in nature. Think about your personal experiences and discuss your own responses to the kinds of events and situations represented in the poem selection.

 ## *My Parents*

- There are implied differences between the persona of the poem and other children (stanza 1). What are these differences?

- What can you infer about the attitude of the persona towards these children?

 ## *Journal*

- The persona claims to be floundering in the 'ocean' cast off by his daughter (lines 4–5). Do you think that this 'ocean' refers to the care and concerns of fatherhood or to the ocean of paper he was trying to write about her? Or both?

- Discuss with your classmates the extended metaphor of swimming and drowning. What is the persona saying about his relationship with his daughter?

- Is this poem really about the persona's daughter, or about the persona himself?

 ## *A Song in the Front Yard*

- The poet is comparing two ways of life: one way is represented by the front yard and the other by the back yard. What are the differences between these two ways of life?

- What are the things about the back yard that the persona of the poem finds attractive?

- Discuss the image of the yard. How does it contribute to the meaning of the poem?

- Consider the title of the poem and discuss its appropriateness to the theme.

- The rhythm and rhyme scheme of the last stanza is different from that used in the other stanzas. Discuss the effectiveness of this stanza in relation to the first three stanzas and to the title and theme of the poem.

p.24 *Fern Hill*

'Fern Hill' (title) – the name of a farm in Wales, UK, on which the poet spent his summer holidays as a boy.

'dingle' (line 3) – a small wooded valley.

'night-jars' (line 25) – nocturnal birds.

'ricks' (line 26) – haystacks.

- Explain what the poet means when he says in line 10 'I was green and carefree …' What is the poem celebrating?

- Why does the poet mention 'Adam and maiden' in line 30? What feelings does he want to express about his experience of waking up on the farm?

- In the final stanza what evidence is there that the childhood experience has faded and the poet is looking back on it from an adult perspective?

p.26 *Counter*

- The word 'counter', which is the title of the poem, is repeated several times in the text of the poem. Examine the different contexts in which it is used and explain the meanings.

- Where do you suppose the 'second row' (lines 10 and 14) is?

- What is 'that distress' referred to in line 11?

p.27 *Overseer: Detention*

'Mau Mau' (line 22) – a nationalist movement of Kenya (1952–60), in which armed peasants revolted against the British Colonial State, as well as its policies and supporters.

'*nèg mawon*' (line 23) – a French-Creole term: literally, 'nèg' translates to 'negro' and 'mawon' translates to 'an unskilled person' or 'a scoundrel'. The idiom refers to a runaway slave.

- Who is the 'Boss' referred to in the poem? Why do you think the poet uses this term?

- Discuss with your classmates how the following phrases enhance or contribute to the meaning of the poem: 'cannon of graffiti' (line 10), 'the walls of his authority' (line 21), 'the repeating shapes/of that lifelong game' (lines 24–25).

- In what ways do you think things 'stayed the same' (line 26)?

- Discuss the significance of the title of the poem.

English Girl Eats Her First Mango

- Why do you think the word 'mellowdramatic' is misspelt the way it is in line 10?

- How many different ways of eating a mango are discussed in the poem? What is *your* favourite way to eat a mango?

- Why does the poet mention 'apple core' in line 60?

- Explain the phrase 'colonisation/in reverse' at the end of the poem.

Walking on Lily Leaves

The lily plant referred to in the poem is the *Victoria Regia* giant water lily, which produces leaves like large, round, flat dishes which float on the water.

'as deftly as tallymen' (line 13) – a tallyman is someone whose job is to count the number of items (usually bunches, bags or bundles of agricultural produce) that have been prepared for export overseas. On wharves, or in the holds of ships, the tallymen step 'deftly' among the produce to count and quantify it.

- Explain in your own words what happens when one of the boys 'walks' on the lily leaves.

- What do the last two lines of the poem reveal about how the adult poet now feels about his childhood game?

Little Boy Crying

- Who is the 'ogre' referred to in line 8?

- Whose thoughts are reflected in stanza 2? Why does the poet use words like 'ogre' and 'giant' (line 8), and 'colossal' (line 9)?

- What is being alluded to in lines 11–13?

- How does the image of the adult presented in stanza 3 differ from that in stanza 2?

School Play

- Explain in your own words why the poet's son prefers the wicked sister to Cinderella.

- Describe how the mother feels about her son's infatuation with the wicked sister and why she feels this way.

- Explain the last three lines of the poem.

The Child Ran Into the Sea

- What is the distinction presented in the description between the sea and the shore?

- What is the attraction of the horizon to the child?

- Discuss the irony in the poem with your classmates.

Wharf Story

In this poem the poet is remembering a time in his childhood when tourists would throw coins into the harbour (careenage) and delight in watching the Bajan boys dive and retrieve them.

- Why does the poet say 'The memory throbs with shame' (line 16)?

- Who does the poet think has replaced the foreign tourists in modern days?

Once Upon a Time

- What things of childhood does the speaking voice of the poem wish for?

- What is implied about growing up and the life of adulthood?

- Can you suggest to whom 'they' and 'their' (lines 2, 4, etc.) refer? Is it made clear in the poem?

- Read lines 1–3 and lines 37–43 carefully. How do you interpret the meaning of these lines?

How Dreams Grow Fat and Die

'*kukumkum*' (line 15) – skinny; a term used in some Jamaican dancehall songs. There is also a suggestion that the sound of the word mimics the sound of bones knocking into each other because there is not enough fat on the body.

'jetés' (line 21) – a ballet term which describes a spring or a leap with one leg forward and the other stretched backwards.

'tutu' (line 25) – a female ballet dancer's short skirt with projecting stiff frills.

- What is the persona's dream in this poem?

- In what ways does the dream die? Find the lines which refer to the death of the persona's dream.

- To whom or to what do you think 'a *kukumkum* orchestra/a herd of bones' refers in lines 15–16?

- Who is the 'You' referred to in stanza 3? Discuss with your classmates the image in the last line of the poem and aspects of the 'You' that it emphasises.

- Does the title help to focus the meaning of the poem? Discuss the ways in which it does or does not do so.

Abra-Cadabra

'narah' (line 12) – a term used in Trinidad and Guyana which refers to a stomach and intestinal disorder caused either by strain from having lifted too heavy an object or from having had a bad fall.

- Find all the specific examples of magic with which the persona credits her mother as performing.

- Do you agree that these examples qualify to be called magic? Explain why or why not.

Aunt Jennifer's Tigers

The tigers in the poem are part of a picture knitted upon a screen by Aunt Jennifer.

- What in the poem is opposed to the 'sleek chivalric certainty' (line 4) of the tigers?

- Explain what is meant or implied by the last two lines of stanza 2.

- In the final stanza, why is the contrast between Aunt Jennifer's hands and the tigers so ironic?

Kanaima/Tiger

'Kanaima' (title) – in Amerindian lore, Kanaima is an avenging spirit that can assume any form it wants as it moves through the forest in pursuit of its human victims.

- What is the quality that distinguishes the 'tiger' from Kanaima?

- Line 18 suggests a contrast in the rubber walk experience before and after the sighting of the 'tiger'. What is this contrast? What does line 18 indicate about the persona's response?

- The persona describes the uncertainty as 'childhood plight' (line 35). Discuss this in the context of what is presented in the final stanza.

p.41

Jamaica Journal

- In line 9 the 'he' in the poem is described as 'too young to understand his day's events' and line 12 refers to 'eyes learning what will later reach his brain'. What are the 'day's events' referred to? What are the implications of these events that he will understand later?

- Explain what you think 'god's unholy sunday-school arrangement' means (line 14).

- Explain the contrast between the boy's experience and the scene he is looking at. What does the fencing symbolise?

- The final stanza suggests some possible futures for the boy. Do you agree that these are inevitable? Discuss the reasons for your response with your classmates.

- Discuss the title of the poem with your classmates. What do you think the poet may wish to convey by the choice of this title?

 p.41

Comfort

- What is it that Mr Sam is making that so beguiles the watching school children? Why does Mr Sam only perform when the children are there to watch?

- What is the persona doing in section III of the poem? Why is the name of the sweet particularly appropriate here?

 p.43

Boy with Book of Knowledge

'Book of Knowledge' (title) – a reference book that was at a time available for use in schools.

'Barbara Frietchie' and 'The Battle Hymn' (line 7), and 'America the Beautiful' (line 8) – these are all described as 'popular, patriotic poems of the Civil War' in America.

- To what does the 'vast pudding of knowledge' (line 13) refer? Why is poetry described as being 'rare as raisins' (line 14)?

- What is the persona's response to poetry? What do the last two stanzas reveal about this response?

PLACES

West Indies, U.S.A.

Cruising at thirty thousand feet above the endless green
the islands seem like dice tossed on a casino's baize,
some come up lucky, others not. Puerto Rico takes the pot,
the Dallas of the West Indies, silver linings on the clouds

5   as we descend are hall-marked, San Juan glitters
like a maverick's gold ring.
                All across the Caribbean
we'd collected terminals – airports are like calling cards,
cultural fingermarks; the hand-written signs at Port-

10   au-Prince, Piarco's sleazy tourist art, the lethargic
contempt of the baggage boys at 'Vere Bird' in St Johns …
And now for plush San Juan.
                But the pilot's bland,
you're safe in my hands drawl crackles as we land,

15   'US regulations demand all passengers not disembarking
at San Juan stay on the plane, I repeat, stay on the plane.'
Subtle Uncle Sam, afraid too many desperate blacks
might re-enslave this *I*sland of the free,
might jump the barbed

20   electric fence around 'America's
back yard' and claim that vaunted sanctuary … 'give me your poor …'
Through toughened, tinted glass the contrasts tantalise;
US patrol cars glide across the shimmering tarmac,
containered baggage trucks unload with fierce efficiency.

25   So soon we're climbing,
                low above the pulsing city streets;
galvanised shanties overseen by condominiums
polished Cadillacs shimmying past Rastas with pushcarts
and as we climb, San Juan's fools-glitter calls to mind

30   the shattered innards of a TV set that's fallen

off the back of a lorry, all painted valves and circuits
the roads like twisted wires,

                    the bright cars, micro-chips.

It's sharp and jagged and dangerous, and belonged to someone else.

Stewart Brown

p.60

Melbourne

Not on the ocean, on a muted bay
Where the broad rays drift slowly over mud
And flathead loll on sand, a city bloats
Between the plains of water and of loam.

5   If surf beats, it is faint and far away;
If slogans blow around, we stay at home.

And, like the bay, our blood flows easily,
Not warm, not cold (in all things moderate),
Following our familiar tides. Elsewhere

10   Victims are bleeding, sun is beating down
On patriot, guerrilla, refugee.
We see the newsreels when we dine in town.

Ideas are grown in other gardens while
This chocolate soil throws up its harvest of

15   Imported and deciduous platitudes,
None of them flowering boldly or for long;
And we, the gardeners, securely smile
Humming a bar or two of rusty song.

Old tunes are good enough if sing we must;

20   Old images, re-vamped *ad nauseam*,
Will sate the burgher's eye and keep him quiet
As the great wheels run on. And should he seek
Variety, there's wind, there's heat, there's frost
To feed his conversation all the week.

25 Highway by highway, the remorseless cars
Strangle the city, put it out of pain,
Its limbs still kicking feebly on the hills.
Nobody cares. The artists sail at dawn
For brisker ports, or rot in public bars.
30 Through much has died here, little has been born.

p.60 *Chris Wallace-Crabbe*

A Place

Alright, someone from Europe might not call it a city.
But if a city mean a place
where ground so hard people stop bury navel string,
and no one looking at a tree can say:
5 'Is my grandfather plant that'; a place
where, no matter how much street lamp light,
all you look out for, all you see, are shadows; a place
where, days and days and days, you only
seeing people you eh really know;
10 and you already starting to accept, believe
that's how it is, that's how life go –
well, if a city is a place just so,
then this plenty-shack-with-couple-condo/jalopy-SUV/spendfast-payslow/
so-it-come-so-it-go/quick-dead/continual-state-of-inbetween-uncertainty
15 is, in some sort of way, i guess, perhaps
        a city

p.61 *Kendel Hippolyte*

A View of Dingle Bay, Ireland

On a prowl for rhyme and reason, I jog
a secondary road between the farms
and there before me like the cantle of a saddle
lies the Bay of Dingle, compliments
5 of American Express and a god

who composes picture postcard views
across creation with indiscriminate
panache, from Caucasus to Caribbean,
from Lake Hakone to Victoria Falls,
10 and leaves it up to us which ones to choose.

From either flank low hills slope down
to a passage wide enough for Viking ships
or a tired dolphin flipping out for pay.
Under a Heaney 'freak of light' a field
15 brindles with cows. On my side is the town

and a pool-pocked strip of sand more littoral
than beach. Will this vista stir my pulse
or of romantic landscapes as with ghettos
can it reluctantly be said, 'If you
20 have seen one, you have seen them all.'

But surely that farmer in his Wellie boots
is the apotheosis of devotion
to the soil! His centuries of ploughing
sillions down could seed the earth. And is
25 his planting more than a putting down of roots?
Ralph Thompson

p.61

Bristol

I leave the cold wet of Bristol. A city of dull
spires and the ostentatious slave money
of the *nouveau riche* who built grand estates
and created a stained empire. The city
5 is changing. Old hints of glory are relics
and the water in the gorge crawls brown,
its concrete lips darkened by rain,
cracked in long fissures. Above is the Clifton
Bridge – that useless act of genius: Egyptian

10   anchors, towers on two sides, the gorge
        below. The marvel of it, the absolute
        hubris of it! The slave money makes you
        think of empire in all things: Ah grandeur!

        I limp along the country lanes. The fat
15   has been falling away each day. Stress
        and the sorrow of a life shattered all eat
        at the sullied flesh. My calf is strained
        by cold and weight. I have lived in a red
        call box, making petitions across the Atlantic
20   each morning before light; an onlooker
        would call it love though it feels like pain
        here in Bristol on these long gloomy days.

        How easy it is to find nothing of poetry
        in a week of patterns: the hills, the castles,
25   the mansions, the bums, the drunken
        students, the moribund theatre, the bland
        food, such dull simplicity. I leave quietly
        at dawn, mutter polite farewells
        to the inquisitive landlady who stands
30   there smiling as if on the verge of thought,
        but so nervous, waiting to be mugged or hugged.

        I say goodbye to her cheapness,
        and think of the furnace I have kept
        burning day after night despite the rules;
35   the dingy room a sauna – her sheets soaked
        in my sweat, and smelling of my tears,
        from long nights haunted by dead slaves,
        their unsettled shadows drifting
        across the Clifton Bridge.

p.61   *Kwame Dawes*

Sonnet Composed upon Westminster Bridge, September 3, 1802

Earth has not anything to show more fair:
Dull would he be of soul who could pass by
A sight so touching in its majesty;
This City now doth, like a garment, wear
5   The beauty of the morning; silent, bare,
Ships, towers, domes, theatres, and temples lie
Open unto the fields, and to the sky;
All bright and glittering in the smokeless air.
Never did sun more beautifully steep
10   In his first splendour, valley, rock, or hill;
Ne'er saw I, never felt, a calm so deep!
The river glideth at his own sweet will:
Dear God! the very houses seem asleep;
And all that mighty heart is lying still!

William Wordsworth

p.62

On the Brooklyn Bridge

I got stuck on the Brooklyn Bridge
and my driver just sat like stone
to the honks and heckles of the horn-head motorist
strapped into his humid summer ride
5   I his passenger cringed
as we slid slowly over this monstrosity
these ark angles of iron that join us to sky-scrapers
islands apart.

I got stuck on the Brooklyn Bridge
10   and remembered you and me cruising
on the old swing bridge back home
romancing the sunshine
caught in the traffic's eye

and the stares of pointing fingers
15 we were not afraid of the gossip then
and when we went roving rumours flew
like black birds in the sky
we always felt free to pause
to park … to piss along any pavement
20 cuss the eye of any hurricane
and felt safe to know that we were home.

In this great city hell is too dark and cold
and the drop from this bridge is death
hell walks all around us
25 aliens trapped on this foreign bridge
in search of fortunes.

p.62   *Winston Farrell*

Castries

(*For John Robert Lee*)

i came upon this town

i came upon this town while she was changing
out of her cotton country Sunday-best
into synthetic pearls and leatherette;
stripping off delicate, eaved French architecture
5 to struggle into high-heeled blocks and functional pillboxes.

Everything was changing:

people, the way they walked, why,
how they waved at you
more and more from a passing car
10 going who the hell knows where – it ceased to matter
after a time. The very language changed.
Even the river festered to a swamp.

The stone lions on the bridge started to lose their teeth.
Then someone closed the wharf from where i used to watch the sunset
15   making miracles with water, a few clouds and a sea-gull.

It all happened so fast:

i was talking Creole love-talk to a girl just down from Morne La Paix –
we finished, bargaining how much it would cost, in American accents.
i've probably resigned myself to it all now
20   except sometimes – like on a day when rain
blurs everything else but memory – i remember
and, in a French ruin overtaken by the coralita
or a girl i knew from Grand Riviere –
Solinah, whose voice still makes a ripple of my name –
25   i glimpse her again, naked and laughing.

Labyrinth

Streets misleading back into each other.
And walk or run, i end
where i began. Lost
in the city's changing ways: the labyrinth.
30   No matter how i turn, it's the wrong way.

Always, i meet the desperate others, the sleek skeletons
that tick to work, tack home
clique-claque to church and back
who balk, always, at my simple, single question.
35   Always, the econometric ordered panicking of people
distracted in the whizz and ritz of their own static
frantic and wandering the maze of licit trafficking
blind to the cloud of furious black flies
that buzz and drip over a something
40   stinking already somewhere beyond the next high-rise block.

Always, all day this white noise
hazes the undersound:
the gnashing of the predator, the victims' groans.
Somewhere within this, the minotaur

45 paces, trampling our scattered bones.

Kendel Hippolyte

45 p.62

The Only Thing Far Away

In this country, Jamaica is not quite as far
as you might think. Walking through Peckham
in London, West Moss Road in Manchester,
you pass green and yellow shops

5 where tie-headwomen bargain over the price
of dasheen. And beside Jamaica is Spain
selling large yellow peppers, lemon to squeeze
onto chicken. Beside Spain is Pakistan, then Egypt,
Singapore, the world … here, strangers build home

10 together, flood the ports with curry and papayas;
in Peckham and on Moss Road, the place smells
of more than just patty or tandoori. It smells like
Mumbai, like Castries, like Princess Street, Jamaica.
Sometimes in this country, the only thing far away

15 is this country.

Kei Miller

p.63

Return

So the street is still there, still melting with sun
still the shining waves of heat at one o'clock
the eyelashes scorched, staring at the distance of the
park to the parade stand, still razor grass burnt and

5 cropped, everything made indistinguishable from dirt
by age and custom, white washed, and the people …
still I suppose the scorpion orchid by the road, that

fine red tongue of flamboyant and orange lips
muzzling the air, that green plum turning fat and
10 crimson, still the crazy bougainvillea fancying and
nettling itself purple, pink, red, white, still the trickle of
sweat and cold flush of heat raising the smell of
cotton and skin … still the dank rank of breadfruit milk,
their bash and rain on steps, still the bridge this side
15 the sea that side, the rotting ship barnacle eaten still
the butcher's blood staining the walls of the market,
the ascent of hills, stony and breathless, the dry
yellow patches of earth still threaten to swamp at the
next deluge … so the road, that stretch of sand and
20 pitch struggling up, glimpses sea, village, earth
bare-footed hot, women worried, still the faces,
masked in sweat and sweetness, still the eyes
watery, ancient, still the hard, distinct, brittle smell of
slavery.

p.63   *Dionne Brand*

Notes and questions

We tend to think of the world in terms of places: the places that we know and visit often; but also the places we read about and hear about and see on TV. Some of the poems here are about places nearby – in the Caribbean – like 'Castries' and the places mentioned in 'West Indies, U.S.A.' Others are about places far away, like 'Melbourne' and 'Bristol' and 'Dingle Bay, Ireland', but they all suggest the excitement of travel and discovery. Think about the places you have visited and also those you hope to visit some day: discover the excitement of thinking and reading about places.

West Indies, U.S.A.

'baize' (line 2) – the green, felt-like material that usually covers gambling tables in casinos.

'hall-marked' (line 5) – a hall-mark is placed by manufacturers on objects made from precious metals.

'maverick' (line 6) – a rebellious, pleasure-seeking adventurer.

'condominiums' (line 27) – expensive apartments, often purchased by outsiders as holiday homes.

- What is the persona saying about the Caribbean by using the language and imagery of the gambling casino in stanza 1?

- The quotation ' "give me your poor …" ' (line 21) is from an inscription on the base of the Statue of Liberty overlooking the approaches to New York Harbour. What is the purpose of quoting this here?

- Note the way that the last line of the poem summarises the experience of the persona and pronounces a final judgement on it.

Melbourne

'Melbourne' (title) – the state capital and most populous city in the Australian state of Victoria. It is the city with the second largest population in Australia.

'ad nauseam' (line 20) – Latin phrase which means 'over and over' or 'enough to make you sick'.

- What is the poet's attitude towards the city of Melbourne? What makes him feel this way?

- Do the last three lines of the poem help the reader to understand the poet's attitude towards the city?

A Place

- What are the things that define a city from the perspective of 'someone from Europe', as presented in lines 1–11?

- From the poet's perspective, what things would qualify a place to be a city?

- Why do you think the phrases in lines 13–14 are run together?

A View of Dingle Bay, Ireland

'American Express' (line 5) – a credit company that issues credit cards on which people charge the goods and services they purchase and then repay the company (American Express) at a later date.

'panache' (line 8) – a dashing manner.

'Heaney' (line 14) – the name of another poet (Seamus Heaney).

'freak of light' (line 14) – a quotation from a poem by Heaney.

'littoral' (line 16) – relating to the shore of a sea, lake or ocean; a coastal or shore region.

'apotheosis' (line 22) – elevation to the rank of a god, or the glorification of a person or thing, or to idealise someone or something.

'sillions' (line 24) – the furrows in ploughed fields.

- In lines 4–10 the poet says that a 'god' composes pictures/scenes of places across the world and leaves it up to 'us' to choose. Who is the 'us' being referred to? What has the persona of the poem chosen?

- In lines 4–5 the persona says that he got his view with 'compliments of American Express'. What do you think he means by this? What is he doing in the poem?

- What is the point of the questions the persona asks in stanza 4?

- 'But surely' (line 21) indicates a change in the trend of thought. What is the point of the observation made in stanza 5?

Bristol

'Bristol' (title) – a city straddling the River Avon in the south-west of England. It has an important maritime history of trade, including the slave trade.

'Clifton Bridge' (lines 8–9) – a landmark suspension bridge across the River Avon and the Avon gorge in Bristol.

- What are the thoughts and feelings of the persona as he leaves the city of Bristol? What is responsible for these feelings?

- What is the persona's attitude towards his landlady as he says goodbye? What does the phrase 'waiting to be mugged or hugged' (line 31) tell us about *her* feelings or attitude?

- Suggest a reason why the persona seems so fixated on slavery and the city's past.

Sonnet Composed Upon Westminster Bridge, September 3, 1802

- We are told that it is early morning. What does the time of day have to do with the type of scene depicted in the poem?

- How do we know that the persona considers this particular perception of the city to be unusual?

- What is 'all that mighty heart' and why is it 'lying still' (line 14)?

- In what way does the image of the 'heart' contrast with the imagery in the rest of the poem?

On the Brooklyn Bridge

'Brooklyn Bridge' (title) – completed in 1883, this bridge connects the New York boroughs of Manhattan and Brooklyn, across the East River.

- Where is the bridge that the poet is remembering in stanza 2? Why did he feel safe there?

- Describe in your own words three important points of contrast between the two bridges in the poem.

Castries

'Castries' (title) – St Lucia's capital city.

'minotaur' (line 44) – in Greek mythology the minotaur was a creature with the head of a bull and the body of a man; its home was in the centre of a labyrinth (maze) in Crete where he was confined by Daedalus; it fed on human flesh and was eventually slain by the god Theseus.

- What are the main differences between the two parts of the poem?

- What causes all the changes mentioned in the first part of the poem?

- How does the poet come to understand his city by the end of the poem?

The Only Thing Far Away

- Why does the poet say that all the places mentioned in lines 6–13 are not far away? In what sense are they not far?

- Considering the examples presented, in what ways do you think 'this country' is far away (lines 14–15)?

Return

- Several details presented in the poem are introduced by the word 'still'. What is the effect of the repetition of this word?

- What is the conclusion that the persona arrives at in the last four lines of the poem? Do you agree with the persona?

PEOPLE AND DESIRES

PEOPLE

Liminal

evening
the late sky is rinsed of cloud
hills are shuddering lightly in a wind
drawing their ruffled burred coats a little tighter round them.
5   this time of day, this light
the mountains have stopped climbing
they seem to slope, heavy dark slumps of land
as though earth herself is letting go.
in the fold and groin and contour of her hills
10   the green is growing into dark
flowers dim, like freckles of a girl becoming woman, leaving
only hints of what they were, tinted on darkness
the veined sky tightens like a stretched skin
sunset dries out in daguerreotype.

15   since childhood i have done this
watched the day end and the night come
and tried to draw a line between them, isolate
the moment, hold it
with my will, the whole bent of my self
20   but i have never: now i seldom try.
still, without intending – following a felt urge –
i can't let many days go by
not watching the sun set.
i distrust the theories and book-answers that I've read on this
25   they may be right, but they may misconstrue me
i only wish mysterious evening light
would, one day, pour its darkening clarity through me.

p.91   *Kendel Hippolyte*

Swimming Chenango Lake

Winter will bar the swimmer soon.
 He reads the water's autumnal hesitations
A wealth of ways: it is jarred,
 It is astir already despite its steadiness,
Where the first leaves at the first
 Tremor of the morning air have dropped
Anticipating him, launching their imprints
 Outwards in eccentric, overlapping circles.
There is a geometry of water, for this
 Squares off the clouds' redundances
And sets them floating in a nether atmosphere
 All angles and elongations: every tree
Appears a cypress as it stretches there
 And every bush that shows the season,
A shaft of fire. It is a geometry and not
 A fantasia of distorting forms, but each
Liquid variation answerable to the theme
 It makes away from, plays before:
It is a consistency, the grain of the pulsating flow.
 But he has looked long enough, and now
Body must recall the eye to its dependence
 As he scissors the waterscape apart
And sways it to tatters. Its coldness
 Holding him to itself, he grants the grasp,
For to swim is also to take hold
 On water's meaning, to move in its embrace
And to be, between grasp and grasping free.
 He reaches in-and-through to that space
The body is heir to, making a where
 In water, a possession to be relinquished
Willingly at each stroke. The image he has torn
 Flows-to behind him, healing itself,

67

Lifting and lengthening, splayed like the feathers
    Down an immense wing whose darkened spread
35 Shadows his solitariness: alone, he is unnamed
    By this baptism, where only Chenango bears a name
In a lost language he begins to construe –
    A speech of densities and derisions, of half-
Replies to the questions his body must frame
40 Frogwise across the all but penetrable element.
Human, he fronts it and, human, he draws back
    From the interior cold, the mercilessness
That yet shows a kind of mercy sustaining him.
    The last sun of the year is drying his skin
45 Above a surface a mere mosaic of tiny shatterings,
    Where a wind is unscaping all images in the flowing obsidian,
The going-elsewhere of ripples incessantly shaping.

Charles Tomlinson

p.91

A Grandfather Sings

A bajhan breaks the dawn.
Grandfather paces a yard swept bald
with care, singing India
into his granddaughter's ear.

5 His voice strains past walls
where time gnaws on long
as a carili vine strung with bitter bulbs
for cleansing bad blood.

He sings the only lullaby he knows –
10 a prayer from his childhood mornings,
his mother veiled at the jhandi
pleading to gods he no longer serves.

He places their language on her tongue
while eyes open wide in cocoa houses
15   that reek the scent of his labour.
He reads understanding in her babble,

hugs her close breathing gratitude
for newness strange as the communion
in her veins makes her another race.
20   One day she will speak her own words.

So he gives the India he remembers
and wonders at the other tightening
in her curls as light rains through leaves,
blessing them with many, many arms.

Jennifer Rahim

p.92

Basil

The boys still slamming their dominoes
outside of Broda's place. Basil,
who use to be a sweet-boy in his day,
starring in the Country & Western
5   dances, use to be a carpenter, he say,
with the best wood in the whole island,
now sits limp and old,
slamming dominoes hard
on the table with three of his partners
10   wearing their crumpled fedoras push back
on their heads. Basil has had 'nough
woman in his day, has drowned his liver
in rum and good company, has lived
all the life he ever cared to live.
15   Now, he has built a long line of dominoes,
holding the last one in his hand, suspended
over the board, knowing that on either end

of that long, white road with its small black dots,
like a map of all the funerals he has attended,
20   it is his turn to play; that no matter what
any of his partners do, they cannot stop him; no matter
how much his children-mothers quarrel tonight
a man don't go home until he ready.

p.92 *Vladimir Lucien*

Cold as Heaven

Before there is a breeze again
before the cooling days of Lent, she may be gone.
My grandmother asks me to tell her
again about the snow.
5   We sit on her white bed
in this white room, while outside
the Caribbean sun winds up the world
like an old alarm clock. I tell her
about the enveloping blizzard I lived through
10   that made everything and everyone the same;
how we lost ourselves in drifts so tall
we fell through our own footprints;
how wrapped like mummies in layers of wool
that almost immobilized us, we could only
15   take hesitant steps like toddlers
toward food, warmth, shelter.
I talk winter real for her,
as she would once conjure for me to dream
at sweltering siesta time,
20   cool stone castles in lands far north.
Her eyes wander to the window,
to the teeming scene of children
pouring out of a yellow bus, then to the bottle
dripping minutes through a tube

25 into her veins. When her eyes return to me,
   I can see she's waiting to hear more
   about the purifying nature of ice,
   how snow makes way for a body,
   how you can make yourself an angel
30 by just lying down and waving your arms
   as you do when you say
   good-bye.
   Judith Ortiz Cofer

p.92

Dennis Street: Daddy

When you had a drink,
or two, or more you cursed
the tyrant President-for-life
in the foulest words. We revelled
5 in this new language
Mommy would have disapproved.

But you sang the sweetest filmi hits
of Mukesh on love and heartbreak
of that time in the fifties you married
10 and your mandolin plucked
the hearts of strangers and neighbours.
And you cried in the molasses dusk
falling silent, then staggering
to bed, 'Lock up boys.'

15 We knew her, then,
understood what she must have felt
putting up with you all those years
as we emptied the Goodyear tyre
ashtray, wiped the ice-bowl rings,
20 crated the coke empties, capped

the half-filled rum bottles
and switched off all lights
to conserve electricity.

p.93 *Sasenarine Persaud*

Hinckson

Faithfully, Hinckson shuffles each afternoon
to the college pool where he knows there's room
for him. Schooled here, he witnessed the pressures
of Depression. Who can deprive him now of simple pleasures?
5   Wrinkled beyond three score and ten,
he first spoke to me in the men's locker: 'When
the Sea Islanders came, they spoke just like you …
Gul … lah, Africa, Yoru …'
He raises a forefinger, doubtfully, to his lips.
10   'It's BAR … BARbados you're from … isn't it?'
He said black folks taught him how to speak.
As a child, he spent more time at nanny's feet
than in his own mother's arms. But now
he has difficulty fitting things he used to know.
15   Now, his last memories are his first.
And I look at him and my heart feels to burst.
What did he think of MLK's death?
Of desegregation? Of the racism that's left?
What were his feelings on the Civil Rights Act?
20   Somehow, I couldn't bring myself to ask.
He stood there painfully ordering his thoughts,
his feet shuffling with afterthoughts.
We'd spoken a dozen times, but he can't remember my name.
'BAR-bados,' he calls me, each time in the same
25   dactylic beat: a child attempting a new word:
a sputtering, one-wing bird.

p.93 *Anthony Kellman*

The Deportee

Barefooted boys gaze at his
so white and so new tee shirt
with the lizard-cool Snoop Dog.
Yes, he is from Stateside with first-
5   hand knowledge of Jay Z
and the poetry of Tupac.
When a dreadlock escapes
the on-backward Kangol,
he touches it with gold-
10   ringed fingers and adjusts
the gold cross as he explains
Shaq's jealousy of Kobe.
His Phat pants' tucked
into untied Timberlands.

15   Pulled from the trench
and stretched on the dam,
the soggy track-suit
makes him a bed of mud.
Above his head, hands,
20   gray and wrinkled as if
wrapped in wet Band-Aids,
are caught by his dreadlocks,
Rolex and AK47 on its sling.
Bulging all-white eyes stare
25   at the sun. A snail clings
to a lobe and feculent scum
oozes from the gaping mouth.
People, hands masking them,
stare at the carrion that robbed,
30   terrorized and carri' on.

Finally, someone breaks the silence:
But he wearin' some really nice boots.
Stanley Niamatali

p.93

Silk Cotton Trees

Secrets of centuries clutched
within their gnarled trunks.

They are silent seers
of ancestors, backs bent in blazing sun,
5   seeding earth to birth young trees,
the backbone of a nation.

When, in the noonday heat,
some girl, shunning the overseer's
pulsing whip, would hide
10   in foliage at their feet

their branches bent
to mark the place where she,
holding within her breast the memory
of one who gave himself to shield her
15   from the hurt of that same whip,
fell to the whim of massa's will.

There in the darkening earth
she buried one stillborn
between the roots.

20   Now the ghosts of all those loves
whose hearts were given, taken, broken
in that place
sigh the wind's silken breath
through the leaves of these
25   silk cotton trees.

p.93

Hazel Simmons-McDonald

Lala: the Dressmaker

Across from Chang's Green Emporium,
at Halfway Tree, near the fish fry sidewalk
where the men now sit to play at winning
crown and anchor – the dress shop circled her.
5   Inch measure of her life's scramble –
mountain range of chequered scraps
scent of fabric satin and taffeta –
on the wheels of the foot machines
tread-treading on the raw edges of
10   parties, teas and mothers' union's socials,
she was drawn into town, moving yard
by yard on the trains of bridal gowns,
fashioning a living from these things.
There was nothing else to do.

15   The rack of finished dresses, hanging, linings out,
concealed the beadwork her fingers were known for.
(A bald pink mannequin stood in the window –
Issa's had made them necessary.)
She, seated behind the children's magic mahogany
20   and glass case cargo of the trade's beads, buttons,
zippers, a bangle, pencil, candle – even fruit,
finished collars. The firm fat of her hands
dissolved by time into a skein of thin brown linen.
One son. No husband. In silence
25   she stitched the distant canefield's cotton trees,
her shame-me-lady face half hidden by the shoulder length
crisp straightened hair. Occasionally, laughter
like a sluice gate crinkled the black black eyes.

Once, before, in the town's taboo, Mohammed's
30   secret raft of tissue paper and bamboo stood among the

indentured ready to float back to him,
the Indian women chanting
'Allah man say husseh'
She earned her name Lala mingling with the chant
35   then
breaking, climbing, tearing at the women's work
to see the forbidden centre of the thing.

And afterwards, the dry red heat of malaria,
journeying, fighting, fighting through the hot cloth
40   covering a sea of seaweed, to the place where
years later, behind the hidden patterns in the stripped
backroom of the shop, between rough walls
across the naked cedar table, she gambled on futures,
staring into the muddled darjeeling leaves
45   calling the good fortunes of the women to life.

When Lala died
in the backroom of the shop
the girlchildren she had clothed,
whose futures she chose from those cupped in her hand
50   unpicked the beaded dresses to find what she hid
stitched in the lining.
They put the beads in the locks of their hair
their needles flashing (dangerous and quick)
collecting the light
55   opening
opening
their laughter strikes the centre of the clock
at Halfway Tree and the flames of the alleys
lick the rotten wooden walls.

p.94   *Honor Ford-Smith*

Fellow Traveller

You hear the rain crossing the valley?
You know it will strike us quite soon?
You know how this damn roof is leaking?
Well, of course you must know.
5   for you holed it yourself
when the wind start to blow
on the day that you said
the damn walls hold you in
and you feel like you dead
10   and you gone on the roof there, to dance.

You said how you were sure
if you climbed right up high
felt the sun right above you,
your hair in the sky,
15   you would see far far.
That the walls block you up,
that the walls 'paw' you in
and you danced and you laughed.

Now, I was afraid you would fall down.
20   You said No, and, So what if I do?
Is just safety you want?
I have things I must see
and I can't keep on thinking about you.

But you knew I would stay here inside it.
25   You knew I would wait for you.
Now I wait and have waited and will wait
but my dancer, the rain's coming in,
and you see how that big storm is brewing?
Where's my shelter?
30   I drowning again?

You see you, dancer,
big smile on your beautiful mouth?
You see you, seeker?
Fix the roof.

35 Or is I moving out.

p.94 *Jane King*

Drought

The woman is barren. And the blackbirds
have had a hard time this year with the drought
and fallen like moths to the field's floor.

The woman is barren. And the city,

5 crawling south like an oil-slick
will soon be around her ankles.

So she sings: 'Will you marry me?
I will go searching under many flat stones
for moisture of the departed rains.'

10 Sings: O world, will you marry me?

The riverbed's dried up completely, the lizards
have taken to the trees, to the high branches.
The cane rolls westwards, burning burning

In the sunset of her time, in the ploughed crater

15 where the woman like a frail apostrophe
dances palely each evening

Among the fallen blackbirds.

p.94 *Wayne Brown*

I Knew a Woman

I knew a woman, lovely in her bones,
When small birds sighed, she would sigh back at them;
Ah, when she moved, she moved more ways than one:
The shapes a bright container can contain!
5   Of her choice virtues only gods should speak,
Or English poets who grew up on Greek
(I'd have them sing in chorus, cheek to cheek).

How well her wishes went! She stroked my chin,
She taught me Turn, and Counter-turn, and Stand;
10   She taught me Touch, that undulant white skin;
I nibbled meekly from her proffered hand;
She was the sickle; I, poor I, the rake,
Coming behind her for her pretty sake
(But what prodigious mowing we did make).

15   Love likes a gander, and adores a goose:
Her full lips pursed, the errant note to seize;
She played it quick, she played it light and loose;
My eyes, they dazzled at her flowing knees;
Her several parts could keep a pure repose,
20   Or one hip quiver with a mobile nose
(She moved in circles, and those circles moved).

Let seed be grass, and grass turn into hay:
I'm martyr to a motion not my own;
What's freedom for? To know eternity.
25   I swear she cast a shadow white as stone.
But who would count eternity in days?
These old bones live to learn her wanton ways:
(I measure time by how a body sways).

p.95   *Theodore Roethke*

Betrothal

Old story. Young girl getting bigger now:
fifteen, tender, good, submissive;
parents want the best for her:
pious, fierce for family and name,
5   and old traditions steeped in race and time.
Goldsmith's son is thirty-four:
had his days, boy, played an eager field,
wants to settle now and take a wife.
Offers house and future safe as gold,
10   cows and coconuts up Essequibo Coast.
The thing is done, families agree:
a marriage is arranged for all to see,
proud and suitable and good for all
except – she's irremediably locked in tears.
15   She will not talk to family or friends
except to say she does not wish to live
if this must be the burden of her days:
not furious but a quiet, downward look.

All are summoned against this stubbornness:
20   old, gentle uncles come, brothers hold her hands,
white-robed pandit shakes his head and warns.
They appeal to me: I see the girl
I knew since parents gave her birth.
She has her story when we sit alone.
25   Young man she saw once by the temple wall:
hardly speak though they meet at festivals.
Hands once touched, and held, and that's enough.
I say the sensible thing I must
but eyes have blazed like that before,
30   storm-light on a sunless shore.
I meet my old, grey saddened friends.
'She is young! What does she know of life!'

Yes, she is young as the new moon,
green as young grass after rain,

35 but what she now has in her heart –
hard as antique mountain stone
sleepless, ancient scythe of stars.
And, yes, she will kill herself
should you bring this goldsmith's son of yours.

p.95

Ian McDonald

The Solitary Reaper

Behold her, single in the field,
Yon solitary Highland Lass!
Reaping and singing by herself;
Stop here, or gently pass!

5 Alone she cuts and binds the grain,
And sings a melancholy strain;
O listen! For the Vale profound
Is overflowing with the sound.

No Nightingale did ever chaunt

10 More welcome notes to weary bands
Of travellers in some shady haunt,
Among Arabian sands:
A voice so thrilling ne'er was heard
In spring-time from the Cuckoo-bird,

15 Breaking the silence of the seas
Among the farthest Hebrides.

Will no one tell me what she sings? –
Perhaps the plaintive numbers flow
For old, unhappy, far-off things,

20 And battles long ago:
Or is it some more humble lay,
Familiar matter of to-day?

Some natural sorrow, loss, or pain,
That has been, and may be again?

25   Whate'er the theme, the Maiden sang
As if her song could have no ending;
I saw her singing at her work,
And o'er the sickle bending; –
I listened, motionless and still;
30   And, as I mounted up the hill,
The music in my heart I bore,
Long after it was heard no more.

p.95

William Wordsworth

She Walks in Beauty

She walks in beauty, like the night
Of cloudless climes and starry skies;
And all that's best of dark and bright
Meet in her aspect and her eyes:
5   Thus mellowed to that tender light
Which heaven to gaudy day denies.

One shade the more, one ray the less,
Had half impaired the nameless grace
Which waves in every raven tress,
10   Or softly lightens o'er her face;
Where thoughts serenely sweet express,
How pure, how dear their dwelling-place.

And on that cheek, and o'er that brow,
So soft, so calm, yet eloquent,
15   The smiles that win, the tints that glow,
But tell of days in goodness spent,
A mind at peace with all below,
A heart whose love is innocent!

p.95

George Gordon Lord Byron

Orchids

I leave this house
box pieces of the five-week life I've gathered.

I'll send them on
to fill spaces in my future life.

5   One thing is left
a spray of orchids someone gave
from a bouquet one who
makes a ritual of flower-giving sent.

The orchids have no fragrance
10   but purple petals draw you
to look at the purple heart.

I watered them once
when the blossoms were full blown
like polished poems.
15   I was sure they'd wilt
and I would toss them out with the five-week litter.

They were stubborn.
I starved them.
They would not die.

20   This morning the bud at the stalk's tip unfurled.

I think I'll pluck the full-blown blooms
press them between pages of memory.

Perhaps in their thin dried transparency

I'll discover their peculiar poetry.
Hazel Simmons-McDonald

p.96

83

My Grandmother

She kept an antique shop – or it kept her.
Among Apostle spoons and Bristol glass,
The faded silks, the heavy furniture,
She watched her own reflection in the brass

5   Salvers and silver bowls, as if to prove
Polish was all, there was no need of love.

And I remember how I once refused
To go out with her, since I was afraid.
It was perhaps a wish not to be used

10   Like antique objects. Though she never said
That she was hurt, I still could feel the guilt
Of that refusal, guessing how she felt.

Later, too frail to keep a shop, she put
All her best things in one long narrow room.

15   The place smelt old, of things too long kept shut,
The smell of absences where shadows come
That can't be polished. There was nothing then
To give her own reflection back again.

And when she died I felt no grief at all,

20   Only the guilt of what I once refused.
I walked into her room among the tall
Sideboards and cupboards – things she never used
But needed: and no finger-marks were there,
Only the new dust falling through the air.

p.96   *Elizabeth Jennings*

The Zulu Girl

When in the sun the hot red acres smoulder
Down where the sweating gang its labour plies
A girl flings down her hoe, and from her shoulder
Unslings her child tormented by flies.

5   She takes him to a ring of shadow pooled
By the thorn-tree: purpled with the blood of ticks,
While her sharp nails, in slow caresses ruled
Prowl through his hair with sharp electric clicks.

His sleepy mouth, plugged by the heavy nipple,
10   Tugs like a puppy, grunting as he feeds;
Through his frail nerves her own deep languor's ripple
Like a broad river sighing through the reeds.

Yet in that drowsy stream his flesh imbibes
And old unquenched, unsmotherable heat –
15   The curbed ferocity of beaten tribes,
The sullen dignity of their defeat.

Her body looms above him like a hill
Within whose shade a village lies at rest,
Or the first cloud so terrible and still
20   That bears the coming harvest in its breast.

Roy Campbell

p.96

The Woman Speaks to the Man who has Employed her Son

Her son was first made known to her
as a sense of unease, a need to cry
for little reasons and a metallic tide
rising in her mouth each morning.
5   Such signs made her know

that she was not alone in her body.
She carried him full term
tight up under her heart.

She carried him like the poor
10   carry hope, hope you get a break
or a visa, hope one child go through
and remember you. He had no father.
The man she made him with had more
like him, he was fair-minded
15   he treated all his children
with equal and unbiased indifference.

She raised him twice, once as mother
then as father, set no ceiling
on what he could be doctor,
20   earth healer, pilot take wings.
But now he tells her he is working
for you, that you value him so much
you give him one whole submachine gun
for him alone.

25   He says you are like a father to him
she is wondering what kind of father
would give a son hot and exploding
death, when he asks him for bread.
She went downtown and bought three
30   and one-third yards of black cloth
and a deep crowned and veiled hat
for the day he draw his bloody salary.

She has no power over you and this
at the level of earth, what she has
35   are prayers and a mother's tears
and at knee city she uses them.
She says psalms for him

she reads psalms for you
she weeps for his soul
40   her eyewater covers you.

She is throwing a partner
with Judas Iscariot's mother
the thief on the left-hand side
of the cross, his mother
45   is the banker, her draw though
is first and last for she still
throwing two hands as mother and father.
She is prepared, she is done. Absalom.

p.97   *Lorna Goodison*

Elegy for Jane

(*My Student, Thrown by a Horse*)

I remember the neckcurls, limp and damp as tendrils;
And her quick look, a sidelong pickerel smile;
And how, once startled into talk, the light syllables leaped for her,
And she balanced in the delight of her thought,
5   A wren, happy, tail into the wind,
Her song trembling the twigs and small branches.
The shade sang with her;
The leaves, their whispers turned to kissing;
And the mold sang in the bleached valleys under the rose.

10   Oh, when she was sad, she cast herself down into such a pure depth,
Even a father could not find her:
Scraping her cheek against straw;
Stirring the clearest water.
My sparrow, you are not here,
15   Waiting like a fern, making a spiny shadow.
The sides of wet stones cannot console me,
Not the moss, wound with the last light.

If only I could nudge you from this sleep,
My maimed darling, my skittery pigeon.
20 Over this damp grave I speak the words of my love:
I, with no rights in this matter,
Neither father nor lover.

p.97 *Theodore Roethke*

Apartment Neighbours

I never see them
yet our lives are linked
by more than walls

the faceless melody
5 of snores of man or mate
the several callers
marked by urgent knock
or crisp sound of rejected foot-
falling on hard paths
10 grass has never known

tinkle of glass
and plates that settle into sinks
swishing the running kitchen water

hiss of the muted phone
15 and late at night
too late
loud hoses washing
whining pet dogs
coaxing with tender tones
20 humaning them
there in our common backyard space
I cannot see

without them seeing me
and forcing me to smile
25 make a connection
break from the learned restraint
I wear in foreign lands

They never see me
yet I long to ease
30 my constant frown
and say
'Evening Miss Evvy, Miss Maisie
Miss Maud …'

p.97 *Velma Pollard*

Koo

The city's streets construct a maze.
i walk them all ways, all hours, but i can't get out.
Yet i know these corners, the veins in the sidewalks,
these old houses that have outlived fires, hurricanes,
5 hurry-get-rich property developers, the rage for progress.
And from a child i've known this
stubborn, greying house on Brazil Street
and in its always open doorway
this stubborn, greying cobbler: Koo,
10 patient as the precise, measured taps of his hammer.
Koo, eking the waxed twine to the hole
he pierces with his awl, drawing the line through
just like when i was small and he had told me:
'There's a right way to everyt'ing.'
15 As i walk past, in mid-life no longer sure about that,
he taps another nail into the sole.
i watch him, hunched still over his last,
pulling the taut twine home, tightening it – a final knot.
Then he replaces hammer, knife, wax, line, awl

20 back on the shelf.
  He is an ikon. Seeing him, I see
  there is a cord i need to find,
  a kind of line – strong, supple, like what cobblers use.
  i need it: to walk the city's inner maze
25 to find the minotaur and yet not lose
  myself.

  Kendel Hippolyte

Abraham and Isaac After

  Some weeks after, Abraham invites Isaac
  To go with him for their usual evening walk.
  Terrified, the child runs and hides.
  At least once a week from an early age
5 Abraham had taken him across the desert
  up into the dry brush hills to survey the land.
  There they would eat dates and raisins
  while he recounted to the boy old tribal stories.

  But after the incident:
10 the boy busies himself; goats to tend to, water
  to fetch, he will go so far as to help the women
  weave cloth, anything to avoid being alone
  with his own father. For ever after he will carry
  the image of himself, arms trussed back, face
15 down on the altar and the suspense of the silver knife.

Lorna Goodison

Notes and questions

These poems bear witness to the variety within our human community and to our abiding interest in the human personality. In many poems the focus is on family and other relationships and interactions, as the poems depict parents, grandparents, spouses, neighbours; a young girl betrothed against her will, a father–son relationship from the bible, a slave-mother's care for her baby and there are also a few solitary figures.

Liminal

'liminal' (title) – this refers to the threshold between two worlds or states of being, in this case daylight and darkness.

'daguerreotype' (line 14) – an early type of photograph in which an impression was taken on a silver plate sensitised by iodine and developed by mercury vapour. The process and the photograph are named after their French inventor Louis Daguerre.

- Note that the first part of the poem (lines 1–14) is an attempt to capture in detail the process of night enveloping the landscape, while the second part (lines 15–27) explains the persona's motive and his fascination for this process.

- Try to explain in your own words what the last two lines of the poem mean.

Swimming Chenango Lake

'Chenango Lake' (title) – a lake in New York State near Colgate University, where the poet, Charles Tomlinson, taught in 1967. The poem is meant, Tomlinson once explained, to echo the ritual ceremonies of native American Indians when they had to cross water. It is about the difference between looking at the water (the mask, the lake) and actually swimming in it (where the mask is removed and the water is experienced more fully).

- 'For to swim is also to take hold/On water's meaning' (lines 25–26). Which of the five senses, would you say, is most involved in this description?

- What, if anything, strikes you about the description of the action of swimming in lines 28–35? Is this how one normally thinks of swimming? What is the reason for the poet's emphasis and presentation of details here?

A Grandfather Sings

'bajhan' (line 1) – a spiritual song.

'jhandis' (line 11) – a small triangular flag, red or saffron-coloured, on a tall bamboo pole, placed outside a house to show that a ceremony of thanksgiving, usually to the Indian deity Hanuman, has been held there. In some cases a yellow and/or white flag is also used in reference to other deities.

- What do the references to the walls, time and the image of the vine in stanza 2 suggest?

- Discuss the meaning of the following phrases:

  - '… newness strange as the communion/in her veins makes her another race' (lines 18–19)

  - '… wonders at the other tightening/in her curls' (lines 22–23).

- 'So he gives her the India he remembers' (line 21). How does the grandfather do this? Find examples presented in the poem.

- Whose might be the 'many, many arms' referred to in the last line of the poem?

Basil

'Basil' (title) – in St Lucian folklore, the name Basil is usually associated with death.

- On the surface, this poem is about a typical Caribbean scene – older men enjoying a game of dominoes in a rum-shop or night spot – but behind this the poem hints at another meaning. What is this meaning?

- Point out the one line that is a simile and is the main clue to the poem's second meaning.

Cold as Heaven

- The poet, Judith Ortiz Cofer, is from Puerto Rico, which is probably the setting of the poem. Quote two brief extracts from the poem that indicate this setting.

- What is the purpose, given the above, of all the references to snow and cold?

- It seems that the persona's grandmother is expected to die soon. How is this reflected in the ending (the last four lines) of the poem?

Dennis Street: Daddy

- Who are the 'We' referred to in the poem, and what do you suppose their relationship was to the drunken older man?

- What excites the boys about the title character of the poem? Do they approve or disapprove of him – or both?

- Who is the woman referred to in the final stanza and how does she influence the boys and their activities?

Hinckson

- What is the main impression you get of Hinckson from lines 1–15? What do you infer has happened to him?

- What are the 'simple pleasures' (line 4) he now derives from life?

- 'And I look at him and my heart feels to burst' (line 16). Why does the persona feel this way?

- Discuss the meaning and significance of the last line of the poem.

The Deportee

'Deportee' (title) – men from the Caribbean who commit crimes in North America are deported to their place of birth, hence the term 'deportee' which is well-known in the region. The first stanza sets out clearly this deportee's familiarity with Black American culture and several of its famous icons.

- What major differences do you discern between the appearance of the deportee in stanza 1 and his appearance in stanza 2?

- What do you think happened to this deportee and why?

Silk Cotton Trees

'gnarled' (line 2) – twisted, knotted, covered with bumps.

'seers' (line 3) – those who 'see', with the suggestion of being able to see into the future and the past.

- Describe in your own words the three instances (in stanzas 3, 4 and 5) of the girl's involvement with the silk cotton tree.

- Is the poem really about trees or about history – and whose history?

Lala: the Dressmaker

'shame-me-lady' (line 26) – Jamaican name for *Mimosa Padica*, a sensitive plant with prickly stems and up to 30 pairs of leaflets on them which collapse and close as soon as they are touched.

- What do the following suggest about Lala:
  - 'the dress shop circled her' (line 4)
  - '... on the wheels of the foot machines ... moving yard/by yard on the trains of bridal gowns' (lines 8–12)?

- What are the things that Lala is described as being good at? Find the lines in the poem that indicate these.

- What are the qualities/personality traits that Lala is presented as having?

- Stanzas 3 and 4 describe two different activities that Lala engaged in. What are these?

- Line 34 states 'She earned her name Lala mingling with the chant'. From your reading of stanza 3, how do you think this happened?

- Discuss the final stanza with your classmates. What does it suggest about Lala's legacy?

Fellow Traveller

- How do the desires of the fellow traveller differ from those of the speaker in the poem?

- What is the conflict presented in the poem?

- Read stanza 4 carefully. What do you think 'it' may refer to in the first line of this stanza? Discuss how the lines in the rest of the stanza support your interpretation.

Drought

- In what way is the woman in the poem like the drought?

- Why does she want to get married?

- Is she a real woman, do you think, and does this matter?

I Knew a Woman

- This is a complex poem full of humorous qualifications, and words and phrases that have more than one meaning. Note how the final lines of each stanza (in parentheses) tend to alter or adjust our perspective of what has gone before.

- Words such as 'rake' (line 12), 'goose' (line 15) and 'loose' (line 17) have connotations (suggested meanings) that are different from their literal meanings. These help construct an undercurrent of sensual/sexual suggestiveness in this poem. Point out two other words or phrases that contribute to this effect.

Betrothal

This poem describes a fairly common situation and reaction to an arranged marriage.

- Do you think the advantages and benefits described in stanza 1 should persuade the girl to accept her suitor?

- 'She has her story ...' (line 24). What exactly is her story? Do you consider this to be sufficient enough to make her defy her family and friends?

- Do you agree with the poet's conclusion and warning in the last two lines of the poem?

The Solitary Reaper

This poem focuses on a young woman in the Scottish Highlands, singing to herself as she reaps the grain with a sickle. The poet is captivated by her singing.

- Line 17 indicates that the poet cannot understand the words the girl is singing. Suggest a reason for this.

- What is it, do you think, that makes the poet so entranced by the singing if he cannot understand the words?

- Discuss the importance of the word 'solitary' in the title. How does this affect the poet's – and the reader's – response to the scene described?

She Walks in Beauty

- Trace the development of the description of the 'she' from stanza 1 to stanza 3. What aspect does each stanza focus on?

- Read the poem again and pay attention to the rhyming pattern. How does this enhance the poem?

Orchids

- Orchids are rare and highly prized flowers that mostly grow as parasites on other trees. Why do you think the persona compares or associates them with poems?

- '… press them between pages of memory' (line 22) refers to the, now rare, habit of pressing flowers by flattening and drying them between the pages of a heavy book. What, according to the poem's last two lines, does the poet hope to achieve by doing this?

My Grandmother

'Salvers' (line 5) – a tray of gold, silver or brass on which drinks, letters, etc. are offered.

- What do you think the first line of the poem means? Discuss in particular '– or it kept her'. Find lines that support your interpretation of these words.

- In what way does 'Polish was all, there was no need of love' (line 6) define the grandmother?

- Why do you think the persona 'felt no grief at all' (line 19) when the grandmother died?

- The speaker of the poem makes a distinction between feelings of 'guilt' and 'grief'. What is the difference between these emotions, as expressed in the poem?

- What do the lines '… things she never used/But needed: and no finger-marks …' (lines 22–23) suggest about the grandmother?

The Zulu Girl

The setting of this poem is a farm in South Africa where a gang of labourers is working in a field.

- Suggest two reasons why the girl 'flings down her hoe' and 'unslings her child' from her shoulder.

- What does stanza 4 say about the attitude of the Zulu people? How is this passed on from the girl to her feeding baby?

- Explain how the final stanza compares the mother and child to the landscape in which they live and work. Why is this important?

The Woman Speaks to the Man who has Employed her Son

'throwing a partner' (line 41) – a method of informal saving, widely practised throughout the Caribbean, where a number of people pay a fixed sum of money each month for a fixed period, with a different member of the group taking the collected total ('drawing a hand') each time.

'Absalom' (line 48) – the son of biblical King David who, under the influence of the traitor Achitophel, plotted against his father and was killed, causing the king profound grief.

- What is the 'work' (lines 21–22) that the son is doing?

- What is the purpose of the first three stanzas, which describe the mother's struggle to give birth to her son and to raise him?

- What is meant by the phrases 'bloody salary' (line 32) and 'knee city' (line 36)?

- How is the reference to 'Absalom' (line 48) appropriate at this point in the poem?

Elegy for Jane

- This poem is written for/in memory of 'My student, Thrown by a Horse'. The poet uses images of birds and associates them with his student. Identify the bird images and say what attributes each one emphasises.

- What is the desire expressed in the final stanza? Discuss the sentiments presented in the last three lines of the poem.

Apartment Neighbours

- This poem describes the strain brought on by the enforced proximity of apartment-living in foreign countries. Point out two references to this sense of discomfort.

- Why is the appeal to the auditory imagination (the sense of hearing) so prominent in this poem?

- How does the life described here contrast with life in the Caribbean? Note the final two lines, which are a quotation from a poem by Kamau Brathwaite, 'The Dust'.

Koo

'ikon' (line 21) – a devotional painting or carving, usually in wood, of Christ or another holy figure (especially in the Eastern Church); or an image or a statue.

'minotaur' (line 25) – in Greek mythology the minotaur was a creature with the head of a bull and the body of a man; its home was in the centre of a labyrinth (maze) in Crete where he was confined by Daedalus; it fed on human flesh and was eventually slain by the god Theseus.

- In what sense do you think the speaker of the poem 'can't get out' (line 2)?

- What lesson does the persona learn from observing Koo?

- What is the significance of the 'cord' (line 22) to the speaker of the poem?

Abraham and Isaac After

Lines 4–8 describe Abraham and Isaac's relationship *before* the incident related in the Bible. The rest of the poem tells of the boy's feelings, and his relationship with his father, *after* the incident.

- Do you find Isaac's reactions, feelings and attitude *after* the incident plausible?

- Discuss with your classmates how you would feel if you had a similar experience with your father.

LOVE

Come Breakfast with Me

Come breakfast with me, love
as I dress in white skirts of pure morning;
as I step lightly upon the grassy hem of the world;
as summer flowers lend the air their perfume
5   and garlands of sunlight adorn me.

Put your glass in my tray; fresh orange fruits
of the day, the early croissant, black coffee
with cream.

Let us sit around white tables of conversation,
10   offering Hegel a roll, inviting Kant to counter.
Let us, wrist upon wrist, finger upon finger,
lips upon chaste lips, sing to each other
with our silent, deep songs,
and our gazes full of birds.

15   Let us recount our dreams;
jewelled swords and innocent lovers,
unintended wounds and democratic energies …

Let us breakfast together, together, love

in wide white skirts of pure morning.
Mahadai Das

p.108

The Lady's-Maid's Song

When Adam found his rib was gone
He cursed and sighed and cried and swore,
And looked with cold resentment on
The creature God had used it for.

5   All love's delights were quickly spent
And soon his sorrow multiplied;
He learned to blame his discontent
On something stolen from his side.

And so in every age we find
10   Each Jack, destroying every Joan,
Divides and conquers womankind
In vengeance for the missing bone;
By day he spins out quaint conceits
With gossip, flattery and song
15   And then at night, between the sheets
He wrongs the girl to right the wrong.

Though shoulder, bosom, lip and knee
Are praised in every kind of art,
Here is Love's true anatomy:
20   His rib is gone; he'll have her heart.
So women bear the debt alone
And live eternally distressed,
For though we throw the dog his bone
He wants it back with interest.

p.108 *John Hollander*

Koriabo

Once in rainy season
when sky and river are one
I pause and smell your rank breath
borne on the wet breeze,
5   and I shiver at the whisper it conveyed
of your age and life and longing.
You whose vast memory
I enter, perhaps as a recent, ephemeral blur,
the touch of boat or body

10   hardly registering, as I watch the wind
        blow across your wet back
        causing goosebumps of exploding raindrops,
        and I think it is such a love
        – and expressed like that –
15   that I long for.

        I exhale audibly
        (a gesture lost in the love-song of the rain)
        and resume paddling.
        I'm comforted by the perception
20   that, like you and the wind
        and the rain, I have somewhere
        to go. And who can say
        that the love that I find
        at the inscrutable end of my journey
25   will not be as shiveringly perfect
        as that cold kiss of the wind
        on your bare, brown back?

 p.108

Mark McWatt

Sonnet 73

        That time of year thou mayst in me behold
        When yellow leaves, or none, or few, do hang
        Upon those boughs which shake against the cold,
        Bare ruined choirs, where late the sweet birds sang.
5   In me thou see'st the twilight of such day
        As after sunset fadeth in the west;
        Which by and by black night doth take away,
        Death's second self, that seals up all in rest.
        In me thou see'st the glowing of such fire,
10   That on the ashes of his youth doth lie,

As the deathbed whereon it must expire,
Consumed with that which it was nourished by.
This thou perceiv'st, which makes thy love more strong,
To love that well which thou must leave ere long.
William Shakespeare

p.108

Nexus

You wear your need for me
like an affliction; some strange disease that overtook you unawares.
This need is your undoing,
5   this can't-wait-to-hear-her-voice-once-more
madness, your frenzy that would force
the hours to leap the two long days
since seeing her and seeing her again.

I am your loss of style:
10   the sad cessation of your old war-cry,
'*Pursuer never, always pursued.*'
I am your dotage, your vulnerable
season. This need defies your old
philosophies, disputes your proven
15   forms of reasoning. You swear sometimes
I am your Nemesis, even.

I fear the day, my love,
when you should think this need
a burden that you cannot bear.

20   Be patient. Here is no sorcery,
no duplicitous entanglement.
The Hand that guided me to you
and you to me is stronger than my own.
A higher wisdom pre-contrives

p.109

25 the meeting of improbabilities.
   So anxious need transformed
   by love may rest at ease.
   Esther Phillips

Close to You Now

   Close to you now
   I talk at the evening sky.
   Maybe that is where your heart is,
   your chest all decorated with stars
5 and the keen scythe blade
   of the crescent moon.

   Ever since I gave up telling to anyone
   but you, I have become so filled
   with love that I used to waste.
10 Now I confess to you straight.
   I ask you questions. I sleep.
   I speak the answers when I wake.

   When I gave up walking
   from door to door with my begging bowl
15 I became conscious that my bowl
   had been always full of the fine gold wheat
   which only the prayerful can see and eat.
   And all the time I was living on leftovers.

   In lie in my bed and cry out to you.
20 I cover myself with a humming tune spread
   which says as it weaves itself
   you, you and only you.
   No one could ever sight up
   the true intentions of this heart.

25   But ever since I stop explaining
      I watch them blow past me like chaff.
      Alone and silent now I hear again
      the coded notes played by the rain
      which dictated the first poems.
30   I want to walk across this green island

      singing like the Guinea woman
      showers, showers of blessing
      until you cover my lips
      and I go silent and still
35   and I will see your face
      and want then for nothing.

p.109 *Lorna Goodison*

Lullaby

      Lay your sleeping head, my love,
      Human on my faithless arm;
      Time and fevers burn away
      Individual beauty from
5   Thoughtful children, and the grave
      Proves the child ephemeral:
      But in my arms till break of day
      Let the living creature lie,
      Mortal, guilty, but to me
10   The entirely beautiful.

      Soul and body have no bounds:
      To lovers as they lie upon
      Her tolerant enchanted slope
      In their ordinary swoon.
15   Grave the vision Venus sends
      Of supernatural sympathy,
      Universal love and hope;
      While an abstract insight wakes

Among the glaciers and the rocks
20   The hermit's sensual ecstasy.

Certainty, fidelity
On the stroke of midnight pass
Like vibrations of a bell,
And fashionable madmen raise
25   Their pedantic boring cry:
Every farthing of the cost,
All the dreaded cards foretell,
Shall be paid, but from this night
Not a whisper, not a thought,
30   Not a kiss nor look be lost.

Beauty, midnight, vision dies:
Let the winds of dawn that blow
Softly round your dreaming head
Such a day of sweetness show
35   Eye and knocking heart may bless,
Find our mortal world enough;
Noons of dryness see you fed
By the involuntary powers,
Nights of insult let you pass
40   Watched by every human love.

W.H. Auden

Hate

Hate swelled up inside me,
Choking me, strangling me,
Hiding me from myself behind it.
I could only stand and watch me as I bellowed and shouted at my friend.

5   I heard me abuse him,
Poison others against him
And do many despicable things.

Then myself forced its way through
And I shook hands and said I was sorry.

10   Hate is a funny thing;
It splits you in two,
One part against the other,
So that you can never win.

 David Eva (aged 13)

Echo

Come to me in the silence of the night;
    Come in the speaking silence of a dream;
Come with soft rounded cheeks and eyes as bright
      As sunlight on a stream;
5   Come back in tears,
O memory, hope, love of finished years.

O dream how sweet, too sweet, too bitter sweet,
    Whose wakening should have been in Paradise,
Where souls brimfull of love abide and meet;
10   Where thirsting longing eyes
        Watch the slow door
That opening, letting in, lets out no more.

Yet come to me in dreams, that I may live
    My very life again though cold in death:
15   Come back to me in dreams, that I may give
      Pulse for pulse, breath for breath:
        Speak low, lean low,
As long ago, my love, how long ago.

 Christina Rossetti

It is the Constant Image of Your Face

It is the constant image of your face
framed in my hands as you knelt before my chair
the grave attention of your eyes
surveying me amid my world of knives
5   that stays with me, perennially accuses
and convicts me of heart's-treachery;
and neither you nor I can plead excuses
for you, you know, can claim no loyalty –
my land takes precedence of all my loves.

10   Yet I beg mitigation, pleading guilty
for you, my dear, accomplice of my heart
made, without words, such blackmail with your beauty
and proffered me such dear protectiveness
that I confess without remorse or shame
15   my still-fresh treason to my country
and hope that she, my other, dearest love
will pardon freely, not attaching blame
being your mistress (or your match) in tenderness.

p.110 *Dennis Brutus*

Notes and questions

The poems in this section deal with different forms and manifestations of love and the relationships in which it is expressed. Several themes associated with love are explored. It may be helpful to make a summary statement that expresses what each poem is about, the theme(s) explored, the poet's treatment of each theme and so forth.

Come Breakfast with Me

'Hegel' and 'Kant' (line 10) – 18th century European philosophers.

- Is the poem really about breakfast? If not, what is its real subject?

- Describe the atmosphere that the poem evokes. What does it tell us about the mood and desires of the poet?

The Lady's-Maid's Song

- Is this poem just fun or is it making a serious (feminist) point? Does it have to be either one or the other?

- Explain what the poet means by 'he'll have her heart' (line 20). Is this the 'interest' referred to in the last line?

Koriabo

'Koriabo' (title) – a tributary of the Barima river in the north-west district of Guyana.

- Who is the persona of this poem speaking to and why?

- Describe in your own words the qualities of the 'love' that the poet longs for in lines 13–15.

Sonnet 73

- Notice the way Shakespeare uses three different metaphors to express the same idea, one in each of the three quatrains (groups of 4 lines) of the sonnet. What is the idea being expressed?

- In Shakespeare's sonnets the couplet (the last two lines) is called 'the whip' because it 'lashes back' or comments on the first 12 lines of the poem. How does the couplet in this sonnet comment on the rest of the poem?

Nexus

- In what ways is the 'need' mentioned in line 1 an 'affliction' (line 2)?

- What do you infer were the 'old philosophies' (lines 13–14) of the person addressed in the poem?

- What is the fear expressed by the speaker of the poem?

- How does the speaker of the poem suggest that the bond with the person addressed may be sustained? Discuss this in the context of the final stanza and the last two lines in particular.

Close to You Now

- Describe the various ways in which the speaker of the poem considers herself close to the 'you' addressed in the poem.

- What do the 'rain' (stanza 5) and 'showers' (stanza 6) symbolise?

- Read the stanzas in which the following lines occur and discuss the possible meanings with your classmates:

    - 'I ask you questions. I sleep./I speak the answers when I wake.' (lines 11–12)

    - '… my bowl/had been always full of the fine gold wheat/which only the prayerful can see and eat./And all the time I was living on leftovers.' (lines 15–18)

    - '… I go silent and still/and I will see your face/and want then for nothing.' (lines 34–36).

- Who do you imagine the 'you' addressed in the poem might be?

Lullaby

This poem attempts, perhaps, to bridge the gap between the values we traditionally assign to body and soul, i.e. the physical pleasures of the body (often associated with sin) and the spiritual virtues of the soul.

- The 'fashionable madmen' with their 'pedantic boring cry' about paying the cost (lines 24–26) are the guardians of moral standards of the society. Why is the persona targeting them?

- Time and mortality are strong arguments in this poem against facile moral judgements. Point out two examples of this.

Hate

- The poet suggests that there are two personalities in this poem. Can you explain the differences in the references to 'me' and 'myself' in the poem?

- Which personality seems to be the genuine self? Does this self experience the hate that is expressed in the poem? If not, what does this self experience?

- Explain the meaning of 'Then myself forced its way through' (line 8).

Echo

In this poem the poet is urging her lover to come back to her.

- Is her lover alive or dead? What evidence for your answer can you find in the poem?

- Where is the 'door' referred to in line 11? Why is it 'letting in' but 'lets out' no one (line 12)?

- What kind of return of her lover does the poet settle for in the final stanza?

It is the Constant Image of Your Face

- Can you explain the nature of the conflict experienced by the persona in this poem?

- For whom is love expressed by the persona of the poem?

- What is the 'treachery' referred to in line 6?

- What is the nature of the 'treason' the persona has committed? Do you agree with the view that it is treason?

- The persona's two loves possess, in his view, a similar quality. What is this quality?

- Explain in your own words the meaning of lines 16–18.

RELIGION

God's Grandeur

The world is charged with the grandeur of God.
　　It will flame out, like shining from shook foil;
　　It gathers to a greatness, like the ooze of oil
Crushed. Why do men then now not reck his rod?
5　Generations have trod, have trod, have trod;
　　And all is seared with trade; bleared, smeared with toil;
　　And wears man's smudge and shares man's smell: the soil
Is bare now, nor can foot feel, being shod.

And for all this, nature is never spent;
10　There lives the dearest freshness deep down things;
And though the last lights off the black West went
　　Oh, morning, at the brown brink eastward, springs –
Because the Holy Ghost over the bent
　　World broods with warm breast and with ah! bright wings.

 Gerard Manley Hopkins

Love [3]

Love bade me welcome; yet my soul drew back,
　　Guilty of dust and sin.
But quick-eyed Love, observing me grow slack
　　From my first entrance in,
5　Drew nearer to me, sweetly questioning
　　If I lacked anything.

'A guest,' I answered, 'worthy to be here.'
　　Love said, 'You shall be he.'
'I, the unkind, ungrateful? Ah my dear,
10　I cannot look on Thee.'
Love took my hand, and smiling, did reply,
　　'Who made the eyes but I?'

'Truth, Lord, but I have marred them; let my shame
    Go where it doth deserve.'
15   'And know you not,' says Love, 'who bore the blame?'
    'My dear, then I will serve.'
'You must sit down,' says Love, 'and taste my meat.'
    So I did sit and eat.

p.120   *George Herbert*

The Last Sign of the Cross

My brother left the Church
with his final sign of the cross
of forehead sweat, tie pin
and shoulder pads of jacket,
5   when the worshippers kissed
white Mary's statue.
My mother laments
that her little boy into whose chest
she rubbed dry oaths
10 of Vick's Vapour rub
has abandoned God,
the little boy whom she
baptized in the name of
      the Father
15   and
      of the Son
who is seated at the right hand
of God, hunched like a faucet
waiting to wash away our sins.
20 She is sorry that her little boy
cannot accept the Holy Spirt.
But he has left, walked out
of the church with its rust, its stone,
its dust, walked beyond his mother's caul
25 of worry in search of a place

that tells his story, touching his shoulders
with his final sign of the cross,
the Holy spirit jockey backing on him
like a *lwa*, a child, an albatross.

p.120

Vladimir Lucien

Jesus is Nailed to the Cross

NAOMI   Well in a way it had
         To come to dis. Is so
         Life stay. If him was just
         Anadda likl madman
5   Passing through, dem wouldn'
         Haffe kill him. Him mussi
         Really God fi true, else
         Him would dead t'ree time
         A'ready. And now dem
10   Going to lick some royal
         Nail into him wrist
         And kill him one more time
         Before him dead. Look
         Samuel. De man whole
15   Body jump each time dem
         Bring de hammer down. Blood
         Running from him two hand
         Like two river. Is lift
         Dem lifting up de cross
20   Now – Samuel, dem nail
         So big him weight going tear
         Him off it when dem drop
         De cross inna de hole.

SAMUEL   Naomi yuh know is
25   Now I see de ting. Dis
         Crucifixion is a

Sacrifice. Dis Golgotha,
Hill of de Skull, come like
De altar for de sacrifice.
30   And de man Jesus is de
Offering. And if him
Is God son fi true den
Any how dem kill him, some
Dread dread things going come
35   Upon dis land. So me
Nah leave yah till him dead,
No matta how it bruk
Up mi old body and
Tear mi soul apart. Mi
40   Time well short. Today me
Must find out which priest is
Really priest. Me haffe know
Who have de truth, who have
De power, who me must
45   Follow – de Pharisee dem
or de Nazarene.

p.121   *Pamela Mordecai*

A Stone's Throw

We shouted out
'We've got her! Here she is!
It's her all right'.
We caught her.
5   There she was –

A decent-looking woman, you'd have said,
(They often are)
Beautiful, but dead scared,
Tousled – we roughed her up
10   A little, nothing much

And not the first time
By any means
She'd felt men's hands
Greedy over her body –
15   But ours were virtuous,
Of course.

And if our fingers bruised
Her shuddering skin,
These were love-bites, compared
20   To the hail of kisses of stone,
The last assault
And battery, frigid rape,
To come
Of right.
25   For justice must be done
Specially when
It tastes so good.

And then – this guru,
Preacher, God-merchant, God-knows-what –
30   Spoilt the whole thing,
Speaking to her
(Should never speak to them)
Squatting on the ground – her level,
Writing in the dust
35   Something we couldn't read.
And saw in her
Something we couldn't see,
At least until
He turned his eyes on us,
40   Her eyes on us,
Our eyes upon ourselves.

We walked away
Still holding stones
That we may throw
45 Another day
Given the urge.
p.121 *Elma Mitchell*

Pied Beauty

Glory be to God for dappled things –
   For skies of couple-colour as a brinded cow;
    For rose-moles all in stipple upon trout that swim;
Fresh-firecoal chestnut-falls; finches' wings;
5   Landscape plotted and pieced – fold, fallow, and plough;
    And áll trádes, their gear and tackle and trim.

All things counter, original, spare, strange;
   Whatever is fickle, freckled (who knows how?)
    With swift, slow; sweet, sour; adazzle, dim;
10 He fathers-forth whose beauty is past change:
           Praise him
p.121 *Gerard Manley Hopkins*

Burnt Offerings

How well the ancestors did this!
They mixed wine with oil
poured libations at the altar
quartered bulls, slaughtered rams
5 dipped wheat in wine, made wafer cakes,
cereal offerings, oil and incense slaked
burnt food for God.

Smoke coiled round each rung of air
ascending,
10   pleasing smell
to cleanse all sin, all guilt.

Then He came
and in the sun's heat climbed this tree
bark stripped
15   flesh ripped
wine drip drop
ping from the vine
on scorched earth.

He gave us
20   wafers dipped in wine
we bring tears
libation
for hearts parched from love's absence.

Thus it has always been
25   endless cycle of sin and shame
repentance, love and
longing.

So it will be till
each gourd fills
30   till hearts' rivers brim
and flow
to green the earth.

I now accept your gift
not bread, not wine
35   but Thee!

Seared in this long day's heat
my heart, burnt fragments of my life
I bring for your redemption.

Hazel Simmons-McDonald

The Convert's Defence

He killed our Brother John
and cooked our Brother John
in a great big pot of oil.
Then he ate our Brother John
5   who came for his salvation.

What say ye?

Yes.
I love Father John.
He was tender.
10   He was sweet.
When he told me of the Christ,
I opened my ear like a child
and let him pour in his sweetness
of salvation and redemption.
15   That was enough,
but he gave me more.

God, he said,
sacrificed his only begotten son
for me to live forever.
20   He gave me Christ's body and blood.
The white body melted
like fat on my tongue.
The thin red blood
tasted like sweet wine.

25 Father John said Christ came
for the salvation of all men.
Father John said he came
for the salvation of me.
I didn't know what to do
30 with Father John until he said
he was a friar.

p.122 *Stanley Niamatali*

Holy Sonnet 14

Batter my heart, three-person'd God, for you
As yet but knock, breathe, shine, and seek to mend;
That I may rise and stand, o'erthrow me, and bend
Your force to break, blow, burn, and make me new.
5 I, like an usurp'd town to another due,
Labour to admit you, but oh, to no end;
Reason, your viceroy in me, me should defend,
But is captiv'd, and proves weak or untrue.
Yet dearly I love you, and would be lov'd fain,
10 But am betroth'd unto your enemy;
Divorce me, untie or break that knot again,
Take me to you, imprison me, for I,
Except you enthrall me, never shall be free,
Nor ever chaste, except you ravish me.

p.122 *John Donne*

Notes and questions

The poems in this section do not deal with religion in a strictly conventional sense. Many of them explore religious customs or beliefs as well as biblical events. Some have references to God/gods but they are not preoccupied solely with religious fervour. You may wish to try writing a summary statement about the theme(s) of each poem.

God's Grandeur

- Pay attention to the poet's use of rhyme in this poem. Can you detect a distinct pattern?

- Point out a few examples of alliteration in the poem and discuss how they contribute to the tone, colour and meaning of the poem.

- What, do you think, is the effect of the repetition of 'have trod' (line 5)?

- To what does the poet attribute the renewal of nature? How does he view man's role in nature?

Love [3]

- Who is the 'love' referred to in this poem?

- Explain in your own words the situation being described in the poem, and why the persona's soul 'drew back' (line 1).

- Which of the following terms best describes the technique used in this poem: personification, allegory or metaphor? Explain your choice.

The Last Sign of the Cross

'*lwa*' (line 29) – the reference in this poem is to a Haitian deity or spirit known as 'loa'; in St Lucia the word 'lwa' means law or rule.

- What, according to the first six lines of the poem, causes the poet's brother to leave the church?

- Is there another reason, suggested in the second half of the poem, for the brother's attitude?

- Explain what you think is meant by the suggestion that the brother left the church 'in search of a place/that tells his story' (lines 25–26).

Jesus is Nailed to the Cross

- What does the use of nation language (dialect) add to this poem?

- Quote four brief extracts which indicate that the speakers find it very painful to watch the scene before their eyes.

- State in your own words the decision that Samuel feels he has to make that day (lines 40–46). On what will this decision be based?

- 'Naomi describes what is happening and Samuel tries to understand and interpret it for the reader.' Is this a fair commentary on the two parts of the poem?

A Stone's Throw

This poem is based on a scene from the New Testament of the Bible in which a woman is about to be stoned. You may read the original account in the Gospel according to John, Chapter 8, Verses 3 to 11.

- Whose is the speaking voice of the poem?

- Can you explain the reference to 'writing in the dust' (line 34)?

- What do the lines in parentheses (lines 7 and 32) indicate?

Pied Beauty

This poem celebrates pied (multi-coloured) beauty in nature. The poet uses a modification of the sonnet form: six lines instead of eight in the first part, and four-and-a-half lines instead of the sestet in the second part.

- Read the poem and check the rhyming pattern. Find and identify the literary devices used. How do these contribute to the euphoric tone and music of the poem?

- What point is the poet making in the second stanza?

Burnt Offerings

- With what are the ancient sacrifices and burnt offerings (lines 1–11) compared in this poem?

- Who is the 'He' that came and brought about this change (line 12)?

- How has the poet reconciled, by the end of the poem, the differing types of 'burnt offerings'? What does the poet suggest as the ultimate reason or purpose for all offerings or sacrifices?

The Convert's Defence

- What is the nature of the accusation in this poem?

- The accuser indicates that Brother John 'came for his salvation' (line 5). The speaker presenting the defence indicates that 'Father John said he came/for the salvation of me' (lines 27–28). Is there any difference between what the accuser and the defender are saying? What is this difference?

- Discuss the last three lines of the poem and the speaker's understanding of 'friar' (line 31).

Holy Sonnet 14

- There are several strong images in this poem, some of them violent. Identify all of these images and discuss why they are used.

- What is the poet asking the 'three-person'd God' to do (line 1)?

- 'I, like an usurp'd town to another due,' (line 5). Who is referred to here by the term 'another'? Explain the simile used in this line.

- 'But am betroth'd unto your enemy' (line 10). Who is the 'enemy'?

- What is the conflict experienced by the persona in this poem?

CONFLICTS AND COMPLICATIONS

RACE AND GENDER

Test Match Sabina Park

Proudly wearing the rosette of my skin
I strut into Sabina
England boycotting excitement bravely,
something badly amiss.

5   Cricket. Not the game they play at Lords,
the crowd – whoever saw a crowd
at a cricket match? – are caged
vociferous partisans, quick to take offence.

England sixty eight for none at lunch.
10   'What sort o battin dat man?
dem kaaan play cricket again,
praps dem should-a-borrow Lawrence Rowe!'

And on it goes, the wicket slow
as the batting and the crowd restless.
15   'Eh white bwoy, how you brudders dem
does sen we sleep so? Me a pay monies
fe watch dis foolishness? Cho!'

So I try to explain in my Hampshire drawl
about conditions in Kent,
20   about sticky wickets and muggy days
and the monsoon season in Manchester
but fail to convince even myself.

The crowd's loud 'busin drives me out
skulking behind a tarnished rosette
25   somewhat frayed now but unable, quite,
to conceal a blushing nationality.

p.138   *Stewart Brown*

124

Theme for English B

The instructor said,

> *Go home and write*
> *a page tonight.*
> *And let that page come out of you –*
5 > *Then, it will be true.*

I wonder if it's that simple?
I am twenty-two, colored, born in Winston-Salem.
I went to school there, then Durham, then here
to this college on the hill above Harlem.
10 I am the only colored student in my class.
The steps from the hill lead down into Harlem,
through a park, then I cross St. Nicholas,
Eighth Avenue, Seventh, and I come to the Y,
the Harlem Branch Y, where I take the elevator
15 up to my room, sit down, and write this page:

It's not easy to know what is true for you or me
at twenty-two, my age. But I guess I'm what
I feel and see and hear, Harlem, I hear you:
hear you, hear me – we two – you, me, talk on this page.
20 (I hear New York, too.) Me – who?

Well, I like to eat, sleep, drink, and be in love.
I like to work, read, learn, and understand life.
I like a pipe for a Christmas present,
or records – Bessie, bop, or Bach.
25 I guess being colored doesn't make me *not* like
the same things other folks like who are other races.
So will my page be colored that I write?
Being me, it will not be white.
But it will be
30 a part of you, instructor.

You are white –
yet a part of me, as I am a part of you.
That's American.
Sometimes perhaps you don't want to be a part of me.
35 Nor do I often want to be a part of you.
But we are, that's true!
As I learn from you,
I guess you learn from me –
although you're older – and white –
40 and somewhat more free.

This is my page for English B.

p.138
Langston Hughes

Vendor

Bunches of coconuts
at the side of the road
and a gate locked behind
them. Then after two days
5 of no takers, a sign marked, 'Free'.

You know what free is, Mister?
The right to be decent:
to knock on the door of a neighbour
or two and ask if they would like
10 some coconuts, and (if they do)
open your gate so they could
go inside and get them.

What do you fear? You think
next morning you may have
15 to say, 'Good morning?'
Or your neighbours might expect
an invitation to your house?

Listen, those coconuts you left
at the side of the road aren't free;
20   they're tainted from the root
by your disease, the prejudice
that masks itself as generosity.
Your faceless gesture marks
a man locked in the old contagion
25   of his race – not free, not free at all.
Esther Phillips

p.139

Dinner Guest: Me

I know I am
The Negro Problem
Being wined and dined,
Answering the usual questions
5   That come to white mind
Which seeks demurely
To probe in polite way
The why and wherewithal
Of darkness U.S.A. –
10   Wondering how things got this way
In current democratic night,
Murmuring gently
Over *fraises du bois*,
'I'm so ashamed of being white.'

15   The lobster is delicious,
The wine divine,
And center of attention
At the damask table, mine.
To be a Problem on

20   Park Avenue at eight
Is not so bad.
Solutions to the Problem,
Of course, wait.

Langston Hughes

Dreaming Black Boy

I wish my teacher's eyes wouldn't
go past me today. Wish he'd know
it's okay to hug me when I kick
a goal. Wish I myself wouldn't
5   hold back when an answer comes.
I'm no woodchopper now
like all ancestors.

I wish I could be educated
to the best of tune up, and earn
10   good money and not sink to lick
boots. I wish I could go on every
crisscross way of the globe
and no persons or powers or
hotel keepers would make it a waste.

15   I wish life wouldn't spend me out
opposing. Wish same way creation
would have me stand it would have
me stretch, and hold high, my voice
Paul Robeson's, my inside eye
20   a sun. Nobody wants to say
hello to nasty answers.

I wish torch throwers of night
would burn lights for decent times.
Wish plotters in pyjamas would pray

25 for themselves. Wish people wouldn't
    talk as if I dropped from Mars.

    I wish only boys were scared
    behind bravados, for I could suffer.
    I could suffer a big big lot.
30 I wish nobody would want to earn
    the terrible burden I can suffer.

James Berry

p.139

Caribbean History

    A flower falls on a leaf,
    the forest sleeps, and
    waves are on holiday.
    El Dorado sings of love
5   as Columbus listens
    in a plastic boat.
    Guacanagari flies to New York,
    – Nobody needs the Sargasso.
    Juliet watches soap operas,
10 and wonders where
    real heroes are gone.
    Magdalene stops by a store
    named, 'Apostles' Feet'.
    – What are winged sandals for?
15 Exploring city slums
    in a purple limousine
    Cleopatra examines
    all painted doors.
    Other VIPs visit
20 St. Elsewhere-in-the-Sun
    for rum and water skis.

    There is no oracle,
    only fraudulent cinemas.

Elections come –
25 now and then,
like bowls of free soup.
Old Moses says.
– Democracy works!
Citizens of some lands
30 stare in one-eyed belief.

But rum-jumbies
dance with people, and
– who don't see don't care.

p.139 **Stanley Greaves**

Black

Roomwalls were pastry crusts ovenbaked in a noon sun.
We, black meat, simmered inside, talked proud
of negritude, sipped whisky and bitter lemon, rum
though our own, was a trifle vulgar after all.
5 Dulcie our maid, white cap and apron, had eyes full and soft
in a glossy melody of oval brows and lashes,
charcoal beauty of face and body which, with proper clothes,
with proper clothes, mind you,
and straightened hair, would put her par
10 with society blonde and brunette in New York and Paree
we all agreed, all regretted her common maidship,
regretted her fleshly share of early bed in low places.
Meanwhile we simmered and sweated, choked
by cool-climate white collar, pendant necktie, occasional
15 whisky and 'good' jobs fit for old colonial whites.

p.140 **Dennis Craig**

The House Slave

The first horn lifts its arm over the dew-lit grass
and in the slave quarters there is a rustling –
children are bundled into aprons, cornbread

and water gourds grabbed, a salt pork breakfast taken.
5   I watch them driven into the vague before-dawn
while their mistress sleeps like an ivory toothpick.

And Massa dreams of asses, rum and slave-funk.
I cannot fall asleep again. At the second horn,
the whip curls across the backs of the laggards. –

10   sometimes my sister's voice, unmistaken, among them.
'Oh! pray,' she cries, 'Oh! pray!' Those days
I lie on my cot, shivering in the early heat,

and as the fields unfold to whiteness,
and they spill like bees among the fat flowers,
15   I weep. It is not yet daylight.

p.140

Rita Dove

Attention

The lights of the city glide within me
but do not pierce through me with their glitter
deep in me there still persists the black depths
of the black history I hear singing.

5   I have heard of blood that ran in torrents
and of the whip that cracked a thousand times,
of the white man who stood guard on the slaves,
sparks in his eyes and thunder in his voice.

We here are the children of a dense night
10   which is shattered in place by strange cries

rages suppressed for many hundred years
today are globules of our own red blood.

Oh wonderful things, oh cities of light
your lights do not keep company with me
15   within me there still remains the black bass
of the black history I hear singing.

p.140 *Mindelense*

The Sleeping Zemis

He kept the zemis under his bed for years
after the day he came upon them in a cave
which resembled the head of a great stone god,
the zemis placed like weights at the tip of its tongue.

5   Arawaks had hidden them there when they fled,
or maybe the stone god's head was really a temple.
Now under his bed slept three zemis,
wrought from enduring wood of ebony.

The first was a man god who stood erect, his arms
10   folded below his belly. The second was a bird god
in flight. The third was fashioned in the form
of a spade, in the handle a face was carved.

A planting of the crops zemi,
a god for the blessing of the corn,
15   for the digging of the sweet cassava
which requires good science

to render the white root safe food.
And over the fields the john crows wheel
and the women wait for the fishermen
20   to return from sea in boats hollowed from trees.

Under his bed the zemis slept.
Where were they when Columbus
and his men, goldfever and quicksilver
on the brain, came visiting destruction?

25   Man god we gave them meat, fish and cassava.
Silent deity we mended their sails, their leaking
ships, their endless needs we filled even with
our own lives, our own deaths.

Bird god, we flew to the hills,
30   their tin bells tolling the deaths
of our children, their mirrors
foreshadowing annihilation to follow.

Spade god we perished.
Our spirits wander wild and restless.
35   There was no one left to dig our graves,
no guides to point us the way to Coyaba.

He turned them over to the keepers of history,
they housed them in glass-sided caves.
Then he went home to sleep without the gods
40   who had slumbered under his bed for years.

Lorna Goodison

p.140

Booker T. and W.E.B.

'It seems to me,' said Booker T.,
'It shows a mighty lot of cheek
To study chemistry and Greek
When Mister Charlie needs a hand
5   To hoe the cotton on his land,
And when Miss Ann looks for a cook,
Why stick your nose inside a book?'

'I don't agree,' said W.E.B.,
'If I should have to drive to seek
10   Knowledge of chemistry or Greek,
I'll do it. Charles and Miss can look
Another place for hand or cook.
Some men rejoice in skill of hand,
And some in cultivating land,
15   But there are others who maintain
The right to cultivate the brain.'

'It seems to me,' said Booker T.,
'That all you folks have missed the boat
Who shout about the right to vote,
20   And spend vain days and sleepless nights
In uproar over civil rights.
Just keep your moths shut, do not grouse,
But work, and save, and buy a house.'

'I don't agree,' said W.E.B.,
25   'For what can property avail
If dignity and justice fail.
Unless you help to make the laws,
They'll steal your house with trumped-up clause.
A rope's as tight, a fire as hot,
30   No matter how much cash you've got.
Speak soft, and try your little plan,
But as for me, I'll be a man.'

'It seems to me,' said Booker T. –

'I don't agree,'

35   Said W.E.B.

p.140   *Dudley Randall*

The Black Man's Son

At twenty, I loved Lise. She was frail and white.
While I, child of the sun, Alas! too dark for her
Won scarce a glance from those bright eyes.

Yet my mother was as white as Lise.
5   She too had shining eyes of blue;
And when she blushed in fear or in delight
Pomegranates seemed to bloom.

Her hair was blond as well, and in the breeze
Veiled a face grown pale with grief.
10   My father was more black than I.
But church had joined their colours in a sacred knot.

And then on her fair breast one saw the sweet antithesis
– a babe as brown and golden as the maize,
As ardent as our tropic sun is, always.

15   Orphaned, I saw Lise and loved her.
Her face grew pale such trembling words to hear
The black man's son struck fear
                in the white folks' daughter.

p.141 *Oswald Durand*

There's a Brown Girl in the Ring

When I speak of this woman I do not mean
To indicate the Muse or abstract queen
But to record the brown fact of her being,
The undiluted blackness of her hair
5   And that I lightly kissed her knee
And how her feet were shy before my stare.

It may be that I praise her memory here
Because she is indeed but allegory
Of meanings greater than herself or me
10   Of which I am instinctively aware;
But may such meanings never be a care
For that fine head, and may my glory be
That blood and brain responded well to slim
Shy feet and smoothest knees and most black hair.

p.141   *Edward Baugh*

Whales

Each Christmas they come
white and blubbery from the frozen North,
strange bloated creatures pale as snow
cruising in vast, unnatural shoals.

5   Whales: the great white whales of myth
and history in all their arrogant splendour.
Flopped ungainly along the sea's edge
or hiding, blistered, under a shadowed palm,

incredibly ugly, somehow, in their difference.
10   Designated a protected species
they are chauffeured around, pampered like babes
and generally kept in the shade.

Few stay long or leave anything behind
except litter and small hostilities.
15   'Peace and Love' we tell them –
the government says we must show respect –

so we smile, sing, play Sambo:
secretly longing for a black Ahab.

p.141   *Stewart Brown*

Goodman's Bay II

*"oh friendly light
oh fresh source of light"*
                        Césaire

Straight to the bush to gather cracked
bottles of beer and rum, shards of seaglass
smoothed by wind and sand. We Haitian

Bahamian descendants, Burial Society
5   flock, crawl through the blue night. Since the light
at dusk is like muslin, we lay the cold

body of this man, then, on the shore
of Goodman's Bay. How he wash here
we don't know, but the workers clearing

10   the beach say, *This him.* John Goodman
he name, originally Jean-Paul Delattre,
brother of Stephen Dillet, first coloured man

in Parliament. Come here on a boat
from Haiti back then, back again,
15   so we jewel the edges of his body

with shattered bottles, then bear him
to the foot of casuarinas in order that his born
silhouette self may freely flash and prance –

luminous shadow lifting from the sand
20   of this beach name after a black man.
Christian Campbell

p.141

Notes and questions

This section explores material that describes attitudes to race, gender relationships and, in the case of one or two poems, class issues. Some of the poems are concerned with concepts like exile and slavery and the consequences of these experiences. Others are concerned with the question of self-identification and what it means to live in a multi-racial world in which colour can still be a barrier between peoples.

Test Match Sabina Park

'Sabina Park' (title) – the home of test cricket in Jamaica.

Lines 3–4 comment on the English style of batting and the grim situation at the crease. However, the poet is also punning on the names of England's opening batsmen at the time the poem was written: Geoff Boycott and Dennis Amiss.

'Lords' (line 5) – a cricket ground in England where test matches are played.

Stanzas 3 and 4 contain examples of Jamaican Creole: 'kaaan' (line 11) – can't; 'Cho!' (line 17) – an expression of annoyance.

- The poet suggests that spectators at Sabina Park are different from those at Lords. In what ways are they different?

- Can you tell what the nationality of the poet is? What clues are given in the poem?

- Explain the meaning of the last stanza.

Theme for English B

'Winston-Salem' and 'Durham' (lines 7–8) – towns in North Carolina, USA.

- The 'college' referred to in line 9 is in New York City as are the streets, places and buildings mentioned in lines 12–14. What do these specific geographical references contribute to the poem?

- The references in line 24 show the persona's wide tastes in music: 'Bessie' refers to Bessie Smith, an American Blues singer; 'bop', to a kind of jazz; 'Bach' to the European classical composer.

- Why do you think the persona mentions the white instructor towards the end of the poem?

p.126 *Vendor*

- How does the poet feel about what is described in the first stanza?

- Why does the poet quarrel with the man getting rid of the coconuts?

- Explain in your own words the argument of the final stanza. Do you agree with the poet's attitude and conclusion?

p.127 *Dinner Guest: Me*

- In what ways does the persona consider himself to be a problem?

- What do you imagine is the difference between the 'Problem' referred to in lines 19–21 and the 'Problem' mentioned in line 22? How does the speaker of the poem indicate this difference in the rest of the poem?

p.128 *Dreaming Black Boy*

'torch throwers of night' (line 22) – possibly a reference to the Ku Klux Klan but also more generally to all destructive groups that engage in such actions.

- In expressing his wishes for different things, the persona of the poem is at the same time lamenting certain attitudes or behaviours. For each wish or set of wishes in each stanza, find one or two words, other than those used in the poem, which describe exactly what the boy is longing for.

- How does the last stanza contribute to the overall meaning of the poem? Do you think that the 'burden' (line 31) referred to in the last stanza has been explained in the rest of the poem?

p.129 *Caribbean History*

'El Dorado' (line 4) – the fabled golden city in South America sought and written about by the Spanish Conquistadors and other adventurers like Walter Raleigh.

'Sargasso' (line 8) – a stagnant area of the Atlantic ocean, caught between area currents and supposedly covered with weeds and other marine growths. It might also be a reference to Jean Rhys's novel *Wide Sargasso Sea*. The other references are to various icons of western history and contemporary popular culture.

- Is the persona merely showing off, with all of these allusions, or do they tell us something about the Caribbean and its history?

- What figure of speech is found in the middle of stanza 3 and what does it tell us about the persona's attitude towards Caribbean politics?

- What does the last stanza mean?

p.130

Black

- What is the attitude of the 'we' in this poem?

- What is it about Dulcie's 'maidship' (line 11) that is regretted and why?

- Do you think the speaker of the poem agrees with the attitudes of the 'we' in the poem? Reference specific lines in your discussion to support your response.

p.131

The House Slave

The house slave in this poem lives and works in the plantation house, while the others, including her relatives, are field slaves and are awakened before dawn to work in the cotton fields.

- Why is the experience of the house slave particularly painful?

- Why does she 'shiver in the early heat' (line 12) when the master and mistress are still asleep?

p.131

Attention

- Is the persona of this poem a slave? How do you know?

- Why does the persona still seem to experience the harshness and horrors of slavery?

p.132

The Sleeping Zemis

'zemi' (title) – a carved figure of a god in Amerindian culture.

- What is the poet saying about the Amerindian people in this poem?

- Explain the significance of the word 'sleeping' in the title, along with the repetition of 'slept' and the word 'slumbered' in the body of the poem.

p.133

Booker T. and W.E.B.

Booker T. Washington was an educator and author, and a dominant leader in the African-American community in the late-19th and early-20th centuries. W.E.B. Dubois was an American sociologist, historian and civil rights activist in the United States in the first half of the 20th century.

- What is the argument in the poem all about? Which point of view do you agree with, and why?

- What does 'A rope's as tight, a fire as hot' (line 29) refer to?

The Black Man's Son
`p.135`

- What is the purpose of the detailed description of the mother in stanzas 2 and 3?
- Why is the 'babe' referred to as an 'antithesis' (lines 12–13)?
- What do you think the 'trembling words' (line 16) were?

There's a Brown Girl in the Ring
`p.135`

The ditty from which the title of this poem is taken is the following:

> There's a brown girl in the ring, tra la la la la
>
> There's a brown girl in the ring, tra la la la la
>
> A brown girl in the ring, tra la la la la
>
> For she likes sugar and I like plum
>
> Oh show me your motion, tra la la la la, etc.

- What are the three things about 'this woman' that the poet celebrates?
- '… she is indeed but allegory/Of meanings greater than herself or me' (lines 8–9). What do you think the 'allegory of meanings' may be here?
- What point is being emphasised in the last four lines of the poem?

Whales
`p.136`

'Ahab' (line 18) – a fictional character in Herman Melville's novel *Moby Dick*. He was a ship's captain who dedicated his entire career to pursuing and killing whales.

- What is the poet using the word 'whales' to refer to?
- Do you consider the descriptions of the attitudes and activities in stanzas 3 and 4 to be fair?
- Why are the 'whales' important to the poet's country and government?
- Explain in your own words the last line of the poem.

Goodman's Bay II
`p.137`

- What is the purpose of the activities described in stanzas 1–3?
- Why do the characters (the 'Burial Society') treat the body in the way that they do?
- '… we jewel the edges of his body' (line 15). Why is this ceremony being carried out?
- What does '… in order that his born/silhouette self may freely flash and prance' (lines 17–18) mean?

WAR

Listening to Sirens

Was it the air-raids that I once lived through
listening to sirens, then the bombers' drone
that makes the spring night charter to Corfu
wake me at 2, alarmed, alert, alone?

5   I watch its red light join the clustered stars
in the one bright clearing in the overcast
then plummet to become a braking car's
cornering deserted side-streets far too fast.

My lilac purples as the headlamps pass

10   and waft it in, that same lilac smell
that once was used to sweeten mustard gas
and induce men to inhale the fumes of hell.
A thin man from that War who lived round here
used to go berserk on nights like these,

15   cower, scream, and crap his pants with fear
whenever he scented lilac on the breeze.

Senses that have been blighted in this way
or dulled by dark winter long for the warm South,
some place we hollow out for holiday,

20   and nothing spoils the white wine in the mouth.
I drag my senses back into the dark
and think of those pale Geordies on their flight.
I'll still be oblivious when they disembark
dazzled by the blue and the bright light.

p.150 *Tony Harrison*

142

Anthem for Doomed Youth

What passing-bells for these who die as cattle?
   – Only the monstrous anger of the guns.
   Only the stuttering rifles' rapid rattle
Can patter out their hasty orisons.
5   No mockeries now for them; no prayers nor bells;
   Nor any voice of mourning save the choirs, –
The shrill, demented choirs of wailing shells;
   And bugles calling for them from sad shires.

What candles may be held to speed them all?
10   Not in the hands of boys, but in their eyes
Shall shine the holy glimmers of goodbyes.
   The pallor of girls' brows shall be their pall;
Their flowers the tenderness of patient minds,
And each slow dusk a drawing-down of blinds.

p.150
Wilfred Owen

This is the Dark Time, My Love

This is the dark time, my love,
All round the land brown beetles crawl about.
The shining sun is hidden in the sky.
Red flowers bend their heads in awful sorrow.

5   This is the dark time, my love.
It is the season of oppression, dark metal, and tears.
It is the festival of guns, the carnival of misery.
Everywhere the faces of men are strained and anxious.

Who comes walking in the dark night time?
10   Whose boot of steel tramps down the slender grass?
It is the man of death, my love, the strange invader
Watching you sleep and aiming at your dream.

p.150
Martin Carter

Other People

In the first World War they ...
Who were *they*? Who cares anymore? ...
Killed four of my uncles,
So I discovered one day.

5   There were only four on that side of the family
And all swept away in a few bad years
In a war the historians tell us now
Was fought over nothing at all.

Four uncles, as one might say
10   A dozen apples or seven tons of dirt,
Swept away by the luck of history,
Closed off. Full stop.

Four is a lot for uncles,
A lot for lives, I should say.
15   Their chalk was wiped clean off the slate,
The War meant nothing at all.

War needs a lot of uncles,
And husbands, and brothers, and so on:
Someone must *want* to kill them,
20   Somebody needs them dead.

Who is it, I wonder. Me?
Or is it you there, reading away,
Or a chap with a small-arms factory?
Or is it only *they*?

p.150 *Chris Wallace-Crabbe*

144

War

When my young brother was killed
By a mute and dusty shell in the thorny brush
Crowning the boulders of the Villa Verde Trail
On the island of Luzon,

5   I laid my whole dry body down,
Dropping my face like a stone in a green park
On the east banks of the Rhine;

On an airstrip skirting the Seine
His sergeant brother sat like a stick in his barracks
10   While cracks of fading sunlight
Caged the dusty air;

In the rocky rolling hills west of the Mississippi
His father and mother sat in a simple Norwegian parlor
With a photograph smiling between them on the table
15   And their hands fallen into their laps
Like sticks and dust;

And still other brothers and sisters,
Linking their arms together,
Walked down the dusty road where once he ran
20   And into the deep green valley
To sit on the stony bank of the stream he loved
And let the murmuring waters
Wash over their blood-hot feet with a springing crown of tears.

p.151 *Joseph Langland*

Break of Day in the Trenches

The darkness crumbles away.
It is the same old druid Time as ever,
Only a live thing leaps my hand,
A queer sardonic rat,

5   As I pull the parapet's poppy
To stick behind my ear.
Droll rat, they would shoot you if they knew
Your cosmopolitan sympathies
(And God knows what antipathies).
10   Now you have touched this English hand
You will do the same to a German
Soon, no doubt, if it be your pleasure
To cross the sleeping green between.
It seems you inwardly grin as you pass
15   Strong eyes, fine limbs, haughty athletes,
Less chanced than you for life,
Bonds to the whims of murder,
Sprawled in the bowels of the earth,
The torn fields of France.
20   What do you see in our eyes
At the shrieking iron and flame
Hurled through still heavens?
What quaver – what heart aghast?
Poppies whose roots are in man's veins
25   Drop, and are ever dropping;
But mine in my ear is safe –
Just a little white with the dust.

Isaac Rosenberg

Poem

Come, brother, and tell me your life
come, show me the marks of revolt
    which the enemy left on your body

Come, say to me 'here
5   my hands have been crushed
because they defended
the land which they own'

'Here my body was tortured
because it refused to bend
10   to invaders'

'Here my mouth was wounded
because it dared to sing
my people's freedom'

Come, brother, and tell me your life,
15   come relate me the dreams of revolt
which you and your fathers and forefathers
dreamed
in silence
through shadowless nights made for love

20   Come tell me these dreams become
war,
the birth of heroes,
land reconquered,
mothers who, fearless,
25   send their sons to fight.

Come, tell me all this, my brother.

And later I will forge simple words
which even the children can understand
words which will enter every house
30   like the wind
and fall like red hot embers
on our people's souls.

In our land
Bullets are beginning to flower.
p.151   *Jorge Rebelo*

Song of War

I shall sleep in white calico;
War has come upon the sons of men
And I shall sleep in calico;
Let the boys go forward,
5   Kpli and his people should go forward;
Let the white man's guns boom,
We are marching forward;
We all shall sleep in calico.

When we start, the ground shall shake;
10   The war is within our very huts;
Cowards should fall back
And live at home with the women;
They who go near our wives
While we are away in battle
15   Shall lose their calabashes when we come.

Where has it been heard before
That a snake has bitten a child
In front of its own mother;
The war is upon us
20   It is within our very huts
And the sons of men shall fight it
Let the white man's guns boom
And its smoke cover us
We are fighting them to die.

25   We shall die on the battlefield
We shall like death at no other place,
Our guns shall die with us
And our sharp knives shall perish with us
We shall die on the battlefield.

p.152   *Kofi Awoonor*

Dulce et Decorum Est

Bent double, like old beggars under sacks,
Knock-kneed, coughing like hags, we cursed through sludge,
Till on the haunting flares we turned our backs
And towards our distant rest began to trudge.
5   Men marched asleep. Many had lost their boots
But limped on, blood-shod. All went lame; all blind;
Drunk with fatigue; deaf even to the hoots
Of tired, outstripped Five-Nines that dropped behind.

Gas! GAS! Quick, boys! – An ecstasy of fumbling,
10   Fitting the clumsy helmets just in time;
But someone still was yelling out and stumbling,
And flound'ring like a man in fire or lime …
Dim, through the misty panes and thick green light,
As under a green sea, I saw him drowning.

15   In all my dreams, before my helpless sight,
He plunges at me, guttering, choking, drowning.

If in some smothering dreams you too could pace
Behind the wagon that we flung him in,
And watch the white eyes writhing in his face,
20   His hanging face, like a devil's sick of sin;
If you could hear, at every jolt, the blood
Come gargling from the froth-corrupted lungs,
Obscene as cancer, bitter as the cud
Of vile, incurable sores on innocent tongues, –
25   My friend, you would not tell with such high zest
To children ardent for some desperate glory,
The old lie: Dulce et decorum est
Pro patria mori.

p.152

Wilfred Owen

149

Notes and questions

The poems in this group deal with the cruelty, the pain and the suffering of war, the weapons, the bravery, the loss (the waste) of life. Notice how in some poems the horrors of war are juxtaposed with images of the beauty and serenity of nature, in order to insist, as it were, that there is an alternative world, at least as large and as real as that of the raging conflict.

p.142

Listening to Sirens

'Geordies' (line 22) – a name for people from the north-east of England, specifically the Newcastle/Durham area.

- Is this a poem about war? Compare this poem with 'Anthem for Doomed Youth'.

p.143

Anthem for Doomed Youth

- Why is the death of the youths likened to that of cattle?

- In what ways is their death contrasted with that of others who die in different circumstances? Why is this contrast made?

- Discuss the significance of the title to the meaning of the poem.

p.143

This is the Dark Time, My Love

This poem is set in British Guiana at the time when the Governor suspended the Constitution and British soldiers were sent in to 'maintain order'.

- This poem juxtaposes guns and soldiers with things of nature, e.g. 'red flowers' (line 4) and 'slender grass' (line 10). Why do you think this juxtaposition is so frequently used in this type of poem?

- What is the effect of the repeated reference to 'my love' in the poem?

- In the last two lines the poet says the 'man of death' is 'aiming at your dream'. What does this mean? What is threatened by the soldiers if not life itself?

p.144

Other People

- This poem laments the loss of the persona's uncles. What is the point being made about their deaths?

- What do the following lines suggest about the persona's reaction to this loss?
  - 'There were only four …/And all swept away in a few bad years' (lines 5–6)
  - 'Four uncles, as one might say/A dozen apples or seven tons of dirt' (lines 9–10)
  - 'Four is a lot for uncles/A lot for lives, I should say' (lines 13–14)
- Why is the phrase 'nothing at all' repeated in the poem (lines 8 and 16)?
- Why is it so difficult to assign blame for the losses the poet feels so keenly?

War

The poet, Joseph Langland, lost his brother during fighting in the Philippines in the Second World War.

- What is the effect of reflecting his brother's death in the thoughts, actions and consciousness of an increasing number of relatives and others, in an increasing number of locations?
- In what ways does the imagery of the last three lines suggest a final calm and closure?

Break of Day in the Trenches

During the First World War the opposing forces in Europe fought in trenches, shooting at each other across vast empty spaces. Isaac Rosenberg, the English poet, was killed in France towards the end of the war in 1918.

- How does the poet use the chance appearance of the rat to make important points about the war and the people who are fighting it?
- What is the point of the contrast being made between the rat and the soldiers in lines 14–16?

Poem

- This poem is an invitation to someone to share information about his life. What specific aspects are selected and why?
- In what ways have the 'dreams of revolt' 'become war' (lines 15–21)?
- Why does the poet wish the words to 'fall like hot embers/on our people's souls' (lines 31–32)?
- What does the last line of the poem mean?

151

Song of War

'calico' (line 1) – a plain, woven textile made from unbleached cotton.

This poem describes the effect of war upon the poet's homeland and people.

- What is the poet saying about 'cowards' (line 11) – those afraid to fight the battle?

- Explain the first three lines of stanza 3. How do they refer to the comment about cowards in stanza 2?

- What does the final stanza seem to be saying about war in general?

Dulce et Decorum Est

Title – From the Latin saying 'Dulce et Decorum Est Pro Patria Mori' – 'It is pleasant and befitting to die for one's country'.

- Notice the contrast between the title (explained above) and the poem itself. What is the poet really saying about fighting in wars for one's country?

THE STRANGE AND THE SUPERNATURAL

The Visit

The keskidee calls stubbornly
from the lianas.
A scramble of brambles

tries the shut door.
5   Nobody in.
Perhaps there's been a gold rush

or something. This is a dead town.
But there's this clock
still ticking. And there's this stable
10   with the fresh smell of dung. Perhaps they'll be back

soon.
So the stranger on the horseback, in formal black,
waited, with an emissary's

patience, while
15   the clock tocked and the stable dried,
the worms gained, and even the door

fell in suddenly, on a clean, well-lighted
place –
then, as great birds came gliding in

20   through the stretched jaws
of the valley,
he was sure, and he turned, slapped leather twice,
and rode off, his slowly cantering horse
raising no echoes nor planting the least

25   hoofprints in the indifferent clay.
Wayne Brown

p.161

Tjenbwa: Night Shift

Some nights he does turn into a pig, a black cat.
Some nights he does squawk his own name
from the lungs of a *malfini*. Some nights
he does undress from his skin, flying out as a flame
5   to see how the night would unfold. And
when his son had get big enough, when the boy
pee finally start to make bold foam in the dirt,
he teach him how to be something more than a man,
teach him the art of transcending his balls, how to wear
10   the legs of cows under his skirt, to be deep and dark
and unanswerable, like the pit-toilet he was now above,
chanting down his poverty with something like wings.
Every night now, going out to work obeah –
making something of himself.
Vladimir Lucien

p.161

My Mother's Sea Chanty

I dream that I am washing
my mother's body in the night sea
and that she sings slow
and that she still breathes.

5   I see my sweet mother
a plump mermaid in my dreams
and I wash her white hair
with ambergris and foaming seaweed.

I watch my mother under water
10   gather the loose pearls she finds,
scrub them free from nacre
and string them on a lost fishing line.

I hear my dark mother
speaking sea-speak with pilot fish,
15 showing them how to direct barks
that bear away our grief and anguish.

I pray my mother breaks free
from the fish pots and marine chores
of her residence beneath the sea,
20 and that she rides a wild white horse.
Lorna Goodison

Mirror

I am silver and exact. I have no preconceptions.
Whatever I see I swallow immediately
Just as it is, unmisted by love or dislike.
I am not cruel, only truthful –
5   The eye of a little god, four-cornered.
Most of the time I meditate on the opposite wall.
It is pink, with speckles. I have looked at it so long
I think it is part of my heart. But it flickers.
Faces and darkness separate us over and over.

10 Now I am a lake. A woman bends over me,
Searching my reaches for what she really is.
Then she turns to those liars, the candles or the moon.
I see her back, and reflect it faithfully.
She rewards me with tears and an agitation of hands.
15 I am important to her. She comes and goes.
Each morning it is her face that replaces the darkness.
In me she has drowned a young girl, and in me an old woman
Rises toward her day after day, like a terrible fish.
Sylvia Plath

A Bat at Dusk

(*For Stewart Brown*)

Quietly, at dusk,
a bat emerges
from the corner of my eye
and I think I see him
5   rip an unworthy thought to shreds
using the last snagged rag of it
to whip himself higher
into the steel-grey vault of sky;
there he examines the emotional freight
10   of coming night – darting between the bales
of primitive fears like a customs clerk,
officious, driven –
telling in the thickening air
the costs of secreted luxuries:
15   sexual fantasies, imaginary feasts,
the delirium of heaven …

But when I looked hard,
trying to see the sum
of his final accounting,
20   I find he has merged his smooth black
into the whole dark cargo
of my mind, become my greatest fear,
as I sense the faint flash of tiny teeth
grinning behind the eyes
25   that can no longer see him.

p.162   *Mark McWatt*

La Belle Dame Sans Merci

First version

O what can ail thee, Knight at arms,
    Alone and palely loitering?
The sedge has withered from the Lake
    And no birds sing!

5   O what can ail thee, Knight at arms,
    So haggard, and so woe begone?
The Squirrel's granary is full
    And the harvest's done.

I see a lily on thy brow
10   With anguish moist and fever dew,
And on thy cheeks a fading rose
    Fast withereth too –

I met a Lady in the Meads,
    Full beautiful, a faery's child
15   Her hair was long, her foot was light
    And her eyes were wild –

I made a Garland for her head,
    And bracelets too, and fragrant Zone
She look'd at me as she did love
20   And made sweet moan –

I set her on my pacing steed
    And nothing else saw all day long
For sidelong would she bend and sing
    A faery's song –

25   She found me roots of relish sweet
    And honey wild and manna dew
And sure in language strange she said
    I love thee true –

She took me to her elfin grot
30   And there she wept and sigh'd full sore,
And there I shut her wild wild eyes
       With kisses four.

And there she lulled me asleep
       And there I dream'd, Ah Woe betide!
35   The latest dream I ever dreamt
       On the cold hill side.

I saw pale Kings, and Princes too
       Pale warriors, death pale were they all;
They cried, La belle dame sans merci
40   Thee hath in thrall.

I saw their starv'd lips in the gloam
       With horrid warning gaped wide,
And I awoke, and found me here
       On the cold hill's side.

45   And this is why I sojourn here
       Alone and palely loitering;
Though the sedge is withered from the Lake
       And no birds sing –

p.162   *John Keats*

Encounter

When I was stumbling
in the dark, confused
and crying out for help,
this friendly fellow seemed amused;

5   and while I fought like anything
to keep the candle lit
he cheerfully reviewed
the guttering of my wit.

10   Astonished that the brother found
my struggle such a treat
I turned the flickering light on him
and glimpsed his cloven feet.

p.163

Mervyn Morris

Ol' Higue

You think I like this stupidness –
gallivanting all night without skin,
burning myself out like cane-fire
to frighten the foolish?

5   And for what? A few drops of baby blood?
You think I wouldn't rather
take my blood seasoned in fat
black-pudding, like everyone else?
And don't even talk 'bout the pain of salt

10   and having to bend these old bones down
to count a thousand grains of rice!

If only babies didn't smell so nice!
And if I could only stop
hearing the soft, soft call

15   of that pure blood running in new veins,
singing the sweet song of life
tempting an old, dry-up woman who been
holding her final note for years and years,
afraid of the dying hum …

20   Then again, if I didn't fly and come
to that fresh pulse in the middle of the night,
how would you, mother,
name your ancient dread?
And who to blame

25   for the murder inside your head …?
      Believe me –
      as long as it have women giving birth
      a poor ol' higue like me can never dead.

Mark McWatt

Notes and questions

The poems in this group range from those that suggest a strange or puzzling event or situation to those that embody our primitive fears, like 'A Bat at Dusk', to those, like 'Ol' Higue', which deal with creatures of folk superstitions, to those that focus on the supernatural and the macabre, like the obeah man in 'Tjenbwa: Night Shift'. Compare the people and events you encounter in these poems with those in tales you have heard along similar lines. Try to decide what it is we find attractive about such themes.

The Visit

'keskidee' (line 1) – a black and yellow bird, a fly-catcher, found on the South American mainland and adjacent islands.

'lianas' (line 2) – thick vines, like ropes, that hang from trees in the tropical forest.

- The town being visited in the poem is empty of humans, but what are some of the details that make this emptiness seem very strange?

- Do you think the person visiting on horseback is a normal living human being? How do the final two lines of the poem help you to answer this question?

Tjenbwa: Night Shift

'Tjenbwa' (title) – in St Lucian French-Creole, this refers to the practice of obeah.

'*malfini*' (line 3) – in St Lucian French-Creole, this refers to a bird, a chicken-hawk.

- According to the poem, how does the obeah man know when his son is old enough to be taught his father's secret trade?

- The last line of the poem indicates the reason for learning the trade of the obeah man. In your own experience, is it simply for status or for material riches, or both?

My Mother's Sea Chanty

'ambergris' (line 8) – a wax-like substance, the colour of ash, found floating in tropical seas. It is used in making perfumes.

'nacre' (line 11) – sometimes called 'mother-of-pearl', this is a smooth, shiny iridescent substance which forms the lining of many sea shells.

- The poem's diction clearly indicates an undersea world. Why does the persona picture her mother in such a world?

- If the persona's mother is dead, how would you interpret the wish for her to 'break free' (line 17) and to 'ride a wild white horse' (line 20)?

p.155

Mirror

In this poem the mirror is addressing you, the reader, describing its role in the lives of people.

- How does the poem make us feel uneasy about the mirror and its role?

- Why does the mirror call itself 'a little god' (line 5)?

- Why is the mirror 'important' to the woman in stanza 2?

- The last two lines of the poem are not to be taken literally. What do they mean?

p.156

A Bat at Dusk

- The bat is described as doing several things in the first stanza. What are these things?

- Why is the thought described as 'unworthy' (line 5)?

- Who is experiencing the 'emotional freight' (line 9)?

- What impression does stanza 1 convey about the persona's reaction to the coming of night?

- What has become of the bat in stanza 2? In what way has the bat become the persona's 'greatest fear' (line 22)?

- What do you think the bat represents in this poem?

p.157

La Belle Dame Sans Merci

'La Belle Dame Sans Merci' (title) – translation from French: The Beautiful Lady Without Pity.

Note that the first two stanzas set the scene and urge the knight to tell his story. The rest of the poem is the knight's story in his own words.

- The form of this poem is that of a ballad. Note the hallmarks of ballad metre: alternating four- and three-stress lines and a rhyme scheme of abcb. Find out as much as you can about the ballad form and see how much of what you learn can be found in this poem.

- Explain in your own words what happened to the knight.

p.158

Encounter

- The poet uses light and darkness, and the brother's differing reactions to these, to indicate moral or, perhaps, spiritual values. How would you explain this further?

- What does 'cloven feet' (line 12) indicate?

p.159

Ol' Higue

Ol' Higue (title) – a version of a vampire, called a 'soucouyant' in Trinidad and some other islands; an old woman who sheds her skin at night, transforms herself into a ball of fire and flies around looking for human victims in order to suck their blood. In some traditions her victims are always babies or very young children.

- The Ol' Higue in this poem is obviously not happy with what she does. In your own words explain why she continues to do it.

- What does the final stanza say about our need to believe in such supernatural beings as the Ol' Higue?

FROM TIME TO ETERNITY

ART, ARTIST, ARTEFACT

A True Poem

Translated by Vernie A. February

A true poem is a thing of awe.
A true poem is a struggle unto death.
A true poem is another land
where one sojourns
5   when one is past death's door.

A true poem is made of words that linger on
when all the others in one's life are washed away:
one single kernel,
but one from which can sprout
10   life all anew.

Stream then all over me
Arusubanya of the world.
Perhaps one day, one day,
my mouth will burst asunder
15   to utter but two words for simple souls
which, as they grow, will sprout ripe stars
which even now I am searching for.

 Trefossa

Photos

The dull red glow
makes liquids
in the shallow pans
seem even more innocent

5   empty paper
the machine's glowing eye

so –
insert the grey transparency
direct it on the paper's blank regard
10   eyes keen in concentration
fingers moving, shaping
sculpting light and shade
the artist's terrible power
to make of what he sees
15   what he wants to be seen
then pass the paper still unmarked
from liquid into liquid
and watch the brutal chemicals
force the reluctant image
20   out of hiding
fashioned not in accordance with its truth
but subject to the power
of those stern hands.

Cynthia Wilson

Bird

(*For Dennis Scott*)

A poem has left its traces
in a thicket of a wild dark region of the mind,
the tip of a branch quivering still
from where the poem, alighting a moment, lifted away
5   suddenly, hearing a poet poaching.

In that clearing to your left, a rustling of syllables,
close? distant? indistinct, stops when you stop
and listen: you do not hear the poem. It hears you.
The silence is the sound
10   of the poem listening.
The poet starts again, approaching
a vined fall of tendrils, trembling like nerved ganglia,
a fibrillating veil across a pathway in a last light.
He parts it, he is touched, he starts again, he enters
15   the thick felt darkness of the mind's wild
and the roar-grunt-chatter-wail-screech-howling of that interior
shrends at the air, straining to shock the skull open, to strike the poet
deaf unto himself.
Under the flailing of your hundred voices, you hunch
20   in, inner, deep, going   to where all sounds,
even the light hush of anticipation,
dim to a silence without weight.
And that is where – sometimes – the bird
will somehow print its cries on air, will sing
25   its darkbright songs towards you from the parted leaves.

p.173   *Kendel Hippolyte*

Swan and Shadow

```
                              Dusk
                         Above   the
                    water  hang  the
                              loud
                             f l i e s
                             Here
                             O so
                             gray
                             then
                    What                        A pale signal  would appear
                    When                   Soon before  its  shadow  fades
                    Where                 Here in this pool of opened eye
                    In   us        No Upon us As at the very edges
                    of where we take  shape  in  the  dark  air
                       this  object  bares  its  image awakening
                         ripples  of  recognition  that  will
                            brush  darkness  up  into  light
        even  after  this  bird this hour both d r i ft  by atop  the  perfect  sad  instant now
                            already  passing  out  of  sight
                         toward  yet-untroubled  reflection
                       this  image bears  its  object darkening
                    into  memorial  shades  Scattered  bits  of
                    light        No of water  Or something across
                    water            Breaking up No Being regathered
                    soon               Yet  by  then  a swan will  have
                    gone                    Yes out  of  mind  into what
                       vast
                       pale
                       hush
                          of  a
                          place
                            past
                    sudden  dark  as
                       if  a  swan
                             sang
```

 John Hollander

Sad Steps

Groping back to bed after a piss
I part thick curtains, and am startled by
The rapid clouds, the moon's cleanliness.

Four o'clock: wedge-shadowed gardens lie
5 Under a cavernous, a wind-picked sky.
There's something laughable about this,

The way the moon dashes through clouds that blow
Loosely as cannon-smoke to stand apart
(Stone-coloured light sharpening the roofs below)

10 High and preposterous and separate –
Lozenge of love! Medallion of art!
O wolves of memory! Immensements! No,

One shivers slightly, looking up there.
The hardness and the brightness and the plain
15 Far-reaching singleness of that wide stare

Is a reminder of the strength and pain
Of being young; that it can't come again,
But is for others undiminished somewhere.

Philip Larkin

p.174

Why I Am Not a Painter

I am not a painter, I am a poet.
Why? I think I would rather be
a painter, but I am not. Well,

for instance, Mike Goldberg
5 is starting a painting. I drop in.
'Sit down and have a drink,' he
says. I drink; we drink. I look
up. 'You have SARDINES in it.'
'Yes, it needed something there.'
10 'Oh.' I go and the days go by
and I drop in again. The painting
is going on, and I go, and the days

go by. I drop in. The painting is
finished. 'Where's SARDINES?'
15   All that's left is just
letters, 'It was too much,' Mike says.

But me? One day I am thinking of
a color: orange. I write a line
about orange. Pretty soon it is a
20   whole page of words, not lines.
Then another page. There should be
so much more, not of orange, of
words, of how terrible orange is
and life. Days go by. It is even in
25   prose, I am a real poet. My poem
is finished and I haven't mentioned
orange yet. It's twelve poems, I call
it ORANGES. And one day in a gallery
I see Mike's painting, called SARDINES.

p.174   *Frank O'Hara*

Sonnet to a Broom

Your frayed teeth must take away the grey dust
fallen from daily reams of urban dreams.
Edges unsullied by your tasks, you sweep
where musty remains of heaven seeped, till
5   you gain only a clean floor of truth
which leaps before Ruth's lace, untainted by
the polluted dust and dirt of weeks.

You retire unpublished to the dark
spaces which my closet keeps, secretly,
10   uncalled, until once more, in despair, I
must dare you now to clear away the grime
accumulated through your absent mime.

Yet unreproachful, you return to use,
efficient though abused, but willing.

 p.174 *Mahadai Das*

Ethics

In ethics class so many years ago
our teacher asked this question every fall:
if there were a fire in a museum
which would you save, a Rembrandt painting
5   or an old woman who hadn't many
years left anyhow? Restless on hard chairs
caring little for pictures or old age
we'd opt one year for life, the next for art
and always half-heartedly. Sometimes
10   the woman borrowed my grandmother's face
leaving her usual kitch to wander
some drafty, half-imagined museum.
One year, feeling clever, I replied
why not let the woman decide herself?
15   Linda, the teacher would report, eschews
the burdens of responsibility.
This fall in a real museum I stand
before a real Rembrandt, old woman,
or nearly so, myself. The colors
20   within this frame are darker than autumn,
darker even than winter – the browns of earth,
though earth's most radiant elements burn
through the canvas. I know now that woman
and painting and season are almost one
25   and all beyond saving by children.

p.174 *Linda Pastan*

Notes and questions

These poems explore the meaning, nature and result of art. They focus on several arts: literature, poetry, photography, painting. See if you can identify values, approaches and techniques that are common to several areas of art.

A True Poem

'Arusubanya' (line 12) – a rapid in the Suriname River, meaning 'it loosens the ribs'.

- Why does the poet carefully describe the idea of what 'a true poem' is?

- What do you think is the reason for the request in the first two lines of stanza 3?

- What is the poet hoping for in stanza 3? Explain the last four lines of the poem.

Photos

'dull red glow' (line 1) – this comes from the safe-light in the photographer's darkroom, where a stronger light would spoil the photosensitive materials exposed.

- The poem describes the process of transferring a negative image ('grey transparency' – line 8) onto paper and causing it to emerge and be fixed there by various chemicals. In this context, can you suggest why the poet uses words like 'terrible' (line 13) and 'brutal' (line 18)?

- What comment do the last three lines make about the nature of art?

Bird

- What is this poem about?

- What does the creative experience of the poet have in common with that of any person trying to find his or her way in natural surroundings?

- Why does the last stanza suggest that silence might be the key to both scenarios?

Swan and Shadow

This is what is known as a concrete poem – or a shape poem.

- How does the shape of the poem help the reader to understand it?

- In what ways is the poem also about time and how the passing of time changes our experience of things, even beautiful things?

- In what way does the title guide the reader to the meaning of the poem?

Sad Steps

'Sad steps' (title) – this is probably an allusion to Sir Philip Sidney's 'Astrophil and Stella' Sonnet 31 (1591): 'With how sad steps, O moon, thou climb'st the skies.'

- Suggest a reason why the poet's own steps may be sad after seeing the moon. Focus especially on the final stanza.

Why I Am Not a Painter

'Mike Goldberg' (line 4) – a New York artist who did silk-screen prints for Frank O'Hara's *Odes* (1960).

- The two longer stanzas are supposedly contrasting the painter and the poet. Do you see any significant differences between the two?

Sonnet to a Broom

- What things are attributed to the broom in stanza 1?

- Why is the dust from 'urban dreams' described as 'grey' (line 1)?

- What does '… you sweep/where musty remains of heaven seeped, till/you gain only a clean floor of truth' (lines 3–5) mean?

- In what ways is the broom 'abused' (line 14)?

Ethics

'Ethics' (title) – the study of questions of right and wrong: moral questions.

- Note that the persona is remembering her childhood up to line 16 and then speaks as an adult in the rest of the poem (lines 17–25). What differences in tone and mood do you see in the two parts of the poem?

- What does the poet mean in the last line: 'all beyond saving by children'?

NOSTALGIA

I Remember, I Remember

I remember, I remember,
The house where I was born,
The little window where the sun
Came peeping in at morn;
He never came a wink too soon,
Nor brought too long a day,
But now, I often wish the night
Had borne my breath away!

I remember, I remember,
The roses, red and white,
The vi'lets , and the lily-cups,
Those flowers made of light!
The lilacs where the robin built,
And where my brother set
The laburnum on his birthday, –
The tree is living yet!

I remember, I remember,
Where I was used to swing,
And thought the air must rush as fresh
To swallows on the wing;
My spirit flew in feathers then,
That is so heavy now,
And summer pools could hardly cool
The fever on my brow!

I remember, I remember,
The fir trees dark and high;
I used to think their slender tops
Were close against the sky:
It was a childish ignorance,

30   But now 'tis little joy
        To know I'm farther off from heav'n
        Than when I was a boy.

Thomas Hood

Himself at Last

This lawyer's niceties paid for his pleasures,
Maintained two sons through university,
Indulged his fat wife's need for jewels.

In his free time he grew anthurium lilies;
5   His wife admired them, passers-by begged for them;
All thought him a true artist at his pastime.

Quibbling was an excellent profession
To this dean of small-island mediocrities;
Until one day a swift, sclerotic stroke
10   Wounded his brain. End of the petty sessions.

His wife has left. His sons have hung *their* shingles.
Now he is what he is, by stern compulsion:
A grower of anthuriums.

Speak praise to heaven for this man's handicaps
15   Which have stripped him at last down to himself.

Slade Hopkinson

Return

(*For Kamau Brathwaite*)

This is the path to new life and to death,
    renaming the earth with familiar sounds,

calling, calling across the green hills
    in three-part harmony, everything jumping,

5   the way the snare springs you back,
        what to do but jump to the pumping sound.

This is the path by the river, now red,
    now reeking of stale bauxite,

the fish are dead, the shrimp are dead,
10   the sea snake dead, the algae dead.

This is the path of new music that calls
    Africa, calls it without knowing,

the pattern of the drums on the skin.
    This is the way the snare makes you jump.

15   My heart beats like a baby's, alert each time
        I embrace dark nights alone.

Here in the stillness, waiting for the crack
    of something, my head pulses in fear.

Then I look for open fields away from predator
20   gunman, a place to wet my body in night dew.

I have returned to plant new grass, new trees,
    and now I know I have returned knowing only

that when death comes, I will be ready,
    for home fires flame in my tender heart, my heart.

p.183   *Kwame Dawes*

South

But today I recapture the islands'
bright beaches: blue mist from the ocean
rolling into the fishermen's houses.
By these shores I was born: sound of the sea

5   came in at my window, life heaved and breathed in me then
with the strength of that turbulent soil.

Since then I have travelled: moved far from the beaches:
sojourned in stoniest cities, walking the lands of the north
in sharp slanting sleet and the hail,
10   crossed countless saltless savannas and come
to this house in the forest where the shadows oppress me
and the only water is rain and the tepid taste of the river.

We who are born of the ocean can never seek solace
in rivers: their flowing runs on like our longing,
15   reproves us our lack of endeavour and purpose,
proves that our striving will founder on that.
We resent them this wisdom, this freedom: passing us
toiling, waiting and watching their cunning declension down to the sea.

But today I would join you, travelling river,
20   borne down the years of your patientest flowing,
past pains that would wreck us, sorrows arrest us,
hatred that washes us up on the flats;
and moving on through the plains that receive us,
processioned in tumult, come to the sea.

25   Bright waves splash up from the rocks to refresh us,
blue sea-shells shift in their wake
and *there* is the thatch of the fishermen's houses, the path
made of pebbles, and look!
Small urchins combing the beaches
30   look up from their traps to salute us:
they remember us just as we left them.

The fisherman, hawking the surf on this side
of the reef, stands up in his boat
and halloos us: a starfish lies in its pool.

35   And gulls, white sails slanted seaward,
      fly into the limitless morning before us.

 p.183

      Kamau Brathwaite

When I Loved You: Four Memories

(*For Linda*)

      I
      When I loved you
      time was with me always
      and I let myself fall
      – that easy, lilting fall into fancy –
5   until I knew nothing at all
      but the sound of your laughter
      and that voice that would call
      across the misty river;
      then the warm breath, the haste
10   of my little heart that beat
      my dreams into a furious pace
      before my distance from our world
      shone like a tear-track down your face,
      when you loved me
15   and time was as ebbing as the sea …

      II
      When I loved you
      along with your old wine
      you offered me
      an atlas of the universe
20   in the shape of your body
      and in return I assured you,
      by subtleties of touch,
      that countless other worlds exist
      beneath the tarnished surfaces
25   of flesh and nature.

Lost in the space of love
we could have wandered forever …
but you touched a frenulum of doubt
and the universe stiffened into flesh,
30   its transubstantial echoes
fading on my tongue
like the taste of wine …

III
When I loved you
we ran with the dark river at night
35   into worlds woven just for us:
oxbows, itabos and lagoons
where love was hard and sharp-edged
with the excitement
of many imagined dangers …
40   until, with the help of
a sudden treason of thought
and a sliver of moon,
I caught a glimpse of your desire
in the rinse of shadows,
45   among flecks of foam like accusing eyes.

This was the danger least expected:
love lived on the dark river
then, in a dark moment of mind,
love died …

IV
50   When I loved you
was it foolish
to want more of you
than flesh or time could give?
When you took yourself away from me
55   for longer than I could bear,
like a foolish child I played God

and made another you
out of words and paper …

How was I to know
60 that this sickness would consume me
until I loved my version of you
better than your real self?
Thirty years later,
in the knowledge that you are safe
65 from me forever,
I'm still making and remaking you
and loving you on paper.

p.184 *Mark McWatt*

Sailing to Byzantium

I
That is no country for old men. The young
In one another's arms, birds in the trees
– Those dying generations – at their song,
The salmon-falls, the mackerel-crowded seas,
5 Fish, flesh, or fowl, commend all summer long
Whatever is begotten, born, and dies.
Caught in that sensual music all neglect
Monuments of unageing intellect.

II
An aged man is but a paltry thing,
10 A tattered coat upon a stick, unless
Soul clap its hands and sing, and louder sing
For every tatter in its mortal dress,
Nor is there singing school but studying
Monuments of its own magnificence;
15 And therefore I have sailed the seas and come
To the holy city of Byzantium.

III

O sages standing in God's holy fire
As in the gold mosaic of a wall,
Come from the holy fire, perne in a gyre,
20   And be the singing-masters of my soul.
Consume my heart away; sick with desire
And fastened to a dying animal
It knows not what it is; and gather me
Into the artifice of eternity.

IV

25   Once out of nature I shall never take
My bodily form from any natural thing,
But such a form as Grecian goldsmiths make
Of hammered gold and gold enamelling
To keep a drowsy Emperor awake;
30   Or set upon a golden bough to sing
To lords and ladies of Byzantium
Of what is past, or passing, or to come.

p.184   *W.B. Yeats*

Notes and questions

All the poems in this small group express a longing – for understanding or enlightenment, for permanence, for release from time, for the simpler world of the past. We all feel a version of this kind of longing from time to time and these poems speak to that experience.

I Remember, I Remember

- Each stanza begins with the phrase 'I remember, I remember' and describes a favourite memory. At the end of stanzas 1, 3 and 4 a regret is expressed. What is the favourite memory? Comment on the corresponding regret.

- Why do you think there is no regret expressed at the end of stanza 2?

- Discuss the meaning of 'My spirit flew in feathers then' (line 21).

Himself at Last

'quibbling' (line 7) – refers to arguing legal questions in court.

'sclerotic stroke' (line 9) – a stroke caused by the hardening or blockage of blood vessels in the brain.

'His sons have hung *their* shingles' (line 11) – means that his sons have all become qualified professionals and have erected signs outside their places of work.

- Why do you think the persona is happy that the man can no longer practise law (lines 14–15)?

Return

Kwame Dawes is a Jamaican poet and this poem is about returning to Jamaica.

- Explain why the persona seems 'alert' (line 15) and fearful, especially of the darkness.

- What is the reason for the persona's return? What is the poem saying about patriotism?

South

- The poet, in exile in northern cities, longs for the sea and his island home. Note that the picture painted of his longed-for seashore is the direct opposite of the details of his present landscape (stanza 2). Is either of these pictures entirely accurate, or has the persona selected and exaggerated the details for a reason? If so, for what reason?

- What are the two roles played by the river in the poem?

- Notice that the poem comes full circle as the final stanza returns to the idyllic landscape of childhood described in stanza 1. What does this tell us about the poet's longing?

When I Loved You: Four Memories

In this poem the poet, Mark McWatt, is remembering (and embellishing) his teenage fantasies about a beautiful girl he met several times on one of Guyana's rivers.

- Explain the following lines in the poem:

  - 'that easy, lilting fall into fancy' (line 4)

  - 'fading on my tongue/like the taste of wine' (lines 31–32)

  - 'This was the danger least expected:/love lived on the dark river/then, in a dark moment of mind,/love died ...' (lines 46–49).

- How does the poet's experience of love change from stanza to stanza?

- Explain the ways in which stanza 4 can be seen to be the climax of all that has gone before it.

Sailing to Byzantium

'Byzantium' (title) – a colony of ancient Greece on a site that later became Constantinople, and later still the modern city of Istanbul in Turkey. In the poem, however, it is an imaginary city – a place in the poet's mind.

- What is it about his own world that makes the aged poet turn to the ideal world that is Byzantium?

- Point out the lines in the poem that indicate the poet is turning away from the real world, from life, and towards eternity.

DEATH

Death Came to See Me in Hot Pink Pants

Last night, I dreamt
that Death came to see me
in hot-pink pants
and matching waistcoat too.

5   He was a beautiful black saga boy.
Forcing open the small door of my wooden cage,
he filled my frame of vision
with a broad white smile,
and as he reached for my throat,

10   the pink sequins on his shoulders
winked at me.

Last night, I dreamt
that Death came to see me in hot-pink pants.
He was a beautiful black saga boy

15   and I hit him with a polished staff
of yellow wood,
and he went down.
But as he reached for me once more,
Laughing, laughing that saga boy laugh,

20   I awoke, holding myself,
unable to breathe.
How beautiful was Death
in hot-pink pants with matching waistcoat too.

 Heather Royes

Mid-Term Break

I sat all morning in the college sick bay
Counting bells knelling classes to a close.
At two o'clock our neighbours drove me home.

In the porch I met my father crying –
5   He had always taken funerals in his stride –
And Big Jim Evans saying it was a hard blow.

The baby cooed and laughed and rocked the pram
When I came in, and I was embarrassed
By old men standing up to shake my hand

10   And tell me they were 'sorry for my trouble',
Whispers informed strangers I was the eldest,
Away at school, as my mother held my hand

In hers and coughed out angry tearless sighs.
At ten o'clock the ambulance arrived
15   With the corpse, stanched and bandaged by the nurses.

Next morning I went up into the room. Snowdrops
And candles soothed the bedside; I saw him
For the first time in six weeks. Paler now,

Wearing a poppy bruise on his left temple,
20   He lay in the four foot box as in his cot.
No gaudy scars, the bumper knocked him clear.

A four foot box, a foot for every year.
Seamus Heaney

For Fergus

When Fergus was dying, I had this fantasy
that when some people die, they ought to leave spaces
like holes in the air where they used to be.

Walking around quite normally, we'd stumble on
these places
5   and choke and gasp in vacuum till the realisation:
Oh! This is where he was. We need true memories, not
just vague traces.

But well before he died, I'd feel a soul-deep irritation
when he would try to drift and they would shake him,
                                        trying to wring
a little more life from him. I wanted him to go with
                            peaceful celebration.

10   I touched his body after they'd roped it in a sheet so
                                        porters could sling
it casually on to a barrow. He was not in it, though we
                                        felt him there
in the room. And walking down a common Castries
                    street, later, I wanted to sing,

feeling his sudden joyous presence everywhere.
From far beyond his death, amazed, he sent a living
        blessing, tingling through the air.

Jane King

Piazza Piece

– I am a gentleman in a dustcoat trying
To make you hear. Your ears are soft and small
And listen to an old man not at all.
They want the young men's whispering and sighing.
5   But see the roses on your trellis dying
And hear the spectral singing of the moon;
For I must have my lovely lady soon,
I am a gentleman in a dustcoat trying.

– I am a lady young in beauty waiting
10   Until my truelove comes, and then we kiss.
But what grey man among the vines is this
Whose words are dry and faint as in a dream?
Back from my trellis, Sir, before I scream!
I am a lady young in beauty waiting.

John Crowe Ransom

It Was the Singing

It was the singing, girl, the singing, it was that
that full my throat and blind my eye
with sunlight. Parson preach good, and didn't
give we no long-metre that day

5   and Judge Hackett make us laugh to hear
how from schooldays Gertie was a rebel
and everybody proud how Sharon talk
strong about her mother and hold her tears.
But the singing was sermon and lesson and eulogy

10   and more, and it was only when we raise
'How Great Thou Art' that I really feel
the sadness and the glory, wave after wave.
Daddy Walters draw a bass from somewhere
we never hear him go before, and Maisie

15   lift a descant and nobody ask her,
but it was the gift they bring, it was
what they had to give and greater
than the paper money overflowing the collection
plate. It was then I know we was people

20   together, never mind the bad-minded and the carry-down
and I even find it in my heart to forgive
that ungrateful Agnes for everything she do me
and I sing and the feelings swelling in my chest
till I had to stop and swallow hard.

25   *Then sings my soul, my saviour God to thee,*
How great thou art, how great thou art …
and we was girls again together, Gertie
and me by the river, and then the singing
was like a wide water and Gertie laughing

30   and waving to me from the other side.
Girl, I can't too well describe it.
Was like the singing was bigger than all of we

and making us better than we think we could be,
and all I asking you, girl, is when
35   my time come to go, don't worry
make no fuss bout pretty coffin
and no long eulogy, just a quiet place
where gunman and drug addict don't haunt,
and if they sing me home like how they sing Gertie
40   I say thank you Jesus, my soul will sleep in peace.
Edward Baugh

p.204

Sylvester's Dying Bed

I woke up this mornin'
'Bout half-past three.
All the womens in town
Was gathered round me.

5   Sweet gals was a-moanin',
'Sylvester's gonna die!'
And a hundred pretty mamas
Bowed their heads to cry.

I woke up little later
10   'Bout half-past fo',
The doctor 'n' undertaker's
Both at ma do'.

Black gals was a-beggin',
'You can't leave us here!'
15   Brown-skins cryin', 'Daddy!
Honey! Baby! Don't go, dear!'

But I felt ma time's a-comin',
And I know'd I's dyin' fast.
I seed the River Jerden

20 A-creepin' muddy past –
    But I's still Sweet Papa 'Vester,
    Yes, sir! Long as life do last!

    So I hollers 'Com'ere, babies,
    Fo' to love yo' daddy right!'
25 And I reaches up to hug 'em –
    When the Lawd put out the light.

    Then everything was darkness
    In a great … big … night.

Langston Hughes

Old Age Gets Up

Stirs its ashes and embers, its burnt sticks

    An eye powdered over, half melted and solid again
    Ponders
    Ideas that collapse
5   At the first touch of attention

    The light at the window, so square and so same
    So full-strong as ever, the window frame
    A scaffold in space, for eyes to lean on

    Supporting the body, shaped to its old work
10 Making small movements in gray air
    Numbed from the blurred accident
    Of having lived, the fatal, real injury
    Under the amnesia

    Something tries to save itself – searches
15 For defenses – but words evade
    Like flies with their own notions

Old age slowly gets dressed
Heavily dosed with death's night
Sits on the bed's edge

20 Pulls its pieces together
Loosely tucks in its shirt
Ted Hughes

Because I Could Not Stop for Death

Because I could not stop for Death –
He kindly stopped for me –
The Carriage held but just Ourselves –
And Immortality.

5 We slowly drove – He knew no haste
And I had put away
My labor and my leisure too,
For His Civility –

We passed the School, where Children strove
10 At Recess – in the Ring –
We passed the Fields of Gazing Grain –
We passed the Setting Sun

Or rather – He passed Us –
The Dews drew quivering and chill
15 For only Gossamer, my Gown –
My Tippet – only Tulle –

We paused before a House that seemed
A Swelling of the Ground –
The Roof was scarcely visible –
20 The Cornice – in the Ground –

Since then – 'tis Centuries – and yet
Feels shorter than the Day
I first surmised the Horses' Heads
Were toward Eternity –

p.204

Emily Dickinson

Requiem

I sing requiem
for the dead, caught in that
mercantilistic madness.

We have not built lasting
5 monuments of severe stone
facing the sea, the watery tomb,

so I call these songs
shrines of remembrance
where faithful descendants

10 may stand and watch the smoke
curl into the sky
in memory of those

devoured by the cold Atlantic.
In every blues I hear
15 riding the dank swamp

I see the bones
picked clean in the belly
of the implacable sea.

Do not tell me
20 it is not right to lament,
do not tell me it is tired.

If we don't who will
recall in requiem
the scattering of my tribe?

25   In every reggae chant
stepping proud against Babylon
I hear a blue note

of lament, sweet requiem
for the countless dead,
30   skanking feet among shell,

coral, rainbow adze,
webbed feet, making as if
to lift, soar, fly into new days.

Kwame Dawes

Death

In death,
the jewelled skin of any fish

will illumine no longer,
will become a slab of spiritless flesh

5   signalling the living no longer,
though light is forever and

the sun stares back at the living
and the dead, steadily

as the look of the undying
10   guards infinity like some rare pearl

in the folds of slackened muscle.
Love will not deny us colour,

variance, rich as a spectrum of cultures.
Knowing that death comes too soon

15   and all will whiten as they pass
out of dappled light,

so memory widens to eternity
as the open stare of any fish in death

draws her light within. Her jewels now,
20   still, within the castle of her skin.
Jennifer Rahim

p.205

Amerindian

I suppose you'd say with truth
No one here looks all that 'right'.
But they settle themselves down.
He was all wrong from start to finish;
5   He squatted in his bed half the time
Paddling a strange bateau.

All his life he knew forests,
Forests and the great rivers.
Why bring him in town to die?
10   His soul is damned that way.
Tribal over-arching heaven
Replaced by rag of sky.

He should have been with brothers,
He should have died with jaguars and stars
15   And a wind rising in the trees.
A last wood-fire comforting
The coming on of cold.

Dream for him a savage vision:
A multitude of years will pass
20   When buildings in this upstart town
Again are lost in sea-drowned grass.
The forest will stay,
Nothing he loved gone down.

Ian McDonald

November

Not that often, but far more often than i would have wanted to,
this year i have deleted numbers, email addresses, names
of those who are beyond the reach of phone calls, computer messages, letters
and the grasping of my voice whether i howl or whisper.
5   Last day of the month, almost 11:30, i lift the calendar's penultimate page
as a man might lift the trapdoor to the cellar in a crumbling house
where every room that he has opened so far
would have been better left shut.
It has been a year in which death was the constant weather,
10   lives slipping into shadow under an overcast of grey terminal conditions,
a drearying intermittent drizzle of sad illnesses,
then the long threatened rain hurling in with an obliterating blur.
i hold the page. One whole month before this year ends.
More rain. More contacts to delete.
15   i wish i could delete the past eleven months.
i hold November still, staring at numbers that begin to blur.
i drop the page. i want to shut the year closed.

Kendel Hippolyte

An Abandoned Bundle

The morning mist
and chimney smoke
of White City Jabavu
flowed thick yellow

5   as pus oozing
     from a gigantic sore.

     It smothered our little houses
     like fish caught in a net.

     Scavenging dogs
10   draped in red bandanas of blood
     fought fiercely
     for a squirming bundle.

     I threw a brick;
     they bared fangs
15   flicked velvet tongues of scarlet
     and scurried away,
     leaving a mutilated corpse –
     an infant dumped on a rubbish heap –
     'Oh! Baby in the Manger
20   sleep well
     on human dung.'

     Its mother
     had melted into the rays of the rising sun,
     her face glittering with innocence
25   her heart as pure as un-trampled dew.

p.205

Oswald Mbuyiseni Mtshali

I Heard a Fly Buzz – When I Died

     I heard a Fly buzz – when I died –
     The Stillness in the Room
     Was like the Stillness in the Air –
     Between Heaves of Storm –

5   The Eyes around – had wrung them dry –
     And Breaths were gathering firm

For that last Onset – when the King
Be witnessed – in the Room –

I willed my Keepsakes – Signed away
10 What portion of me be
Assignable – and then it was
There interposed a Fly –

With Blue – uncertain stumbling Buzz –
Between the light – and me –
15 And then the Windows failed – and then
I could not see to see –

Emily Dickinson

Death of a Steel Bassman

We know that your heart
was cake with dirt, and that
when you beat the big drums
the black steel bloom of your bass
5 was like a big bottom shaking under
the outskirts of Conway, Marchand,
Laventille, and you could hear the music
limping from one note to the other with
your hands like two gunshots stuck in it leg.
10 Hold your *sigawèt of tabak* in your mouth and play
it like low kind thunder that we can touch,
like something from down under, bassline
so free, so low, bass like a big black shadow of sound,
bass like the deep voice of shade cooling
15 down our backs. And we hearing it going on
and on, without sleeping, without rest, a bassline so restless
& so long that it sound far when you beat it,
a baseline so perfect & correct that you feel

like you have to stand up and greet it,

20   so deep sounding like your hands could never reach it,

so far, so long. We had to let you go, had to

send you to meet it.

p.206
Vladimir Lucien

Dead Boy

The little cousin is dead, by foul subtraction,

A green bough from Virginia's aged tree,

And none of the county kin like the transaction,

Nor some of the world of outer dark, like me.

5   A boy not beautiful, nor good, nor clever,

A black cloud full of storms too hot for keeping,

A sword beneath his mother's heart – yet never

Woman bewept her babe as this is weeping.

A pig with a pasty face, so I had said,

10   Squealing for cookies, kinned by poor pretense

With a noble house. But the little man quite dead,

I see the forbears' antique lineaments.

The elder men have strode by the box of death

To the wide flag porch, and muttering low send round

15   The bruit of the day. O friendly waste of breath!

Their hearts are hurt with a deep dynastic wound.

He was pale and little, the foolish neighbors say;

The first-fruits, saith the Preacher, the Lord hath taken;

But this was the old tree's late branch wrenched away,

20   Grieving the sapless limbs, the shorn and shaken.

p.206
John Crowe Ransom

Tropical Death

The fat black woman want
a brilliant tropical death
not a cold sojourn
in some North Europe far/forlorn

5 The fat black woman want
some heat/hibiscus at her feet
blue sea dress
to wrap her neat

The fat black woman want
10 some bawl
no quiet jerk tear wiping
a polite hearse withdrawal

The fat black woman want
all her dead rights
15 first night
third night
nine night
all the sleepless droning
red-eyed wake nights

20 In the heart
of her mother's sweetbreast
In the shade
of the sun leaf's cool bless
In the bloom
25 of her people's bloodrest

the fat black woman want
a brilliant tropical death yes
Grace Nichols

p.207

Do Not Go Gentle into That Good Night

Do not go gentle into that good night,
Old age should burn and rave at close of day;
Rage, rage against the dying of the light.

Though wise men at their end know dark is right,
5   Because their words had forked no lightning they
Do not go gentle into that good night.

Good men, the last wave by, crying how bright
Their frail deeds might have danced in a green bay,
Rage, rage against the dying of the light.

10   Wild men who caught and sang the sun in flight,
And learn, too late, they grieved it on its way,
Do not go gentle into that good night.

Grave men, near death, who see with blinding sight
Blind eyes could blaze like meteors and be gay,
15   Rage, rage against the dying of the light.

And you, my father, there on the sad height,
Curse, bless, me now with your fierce tears, I pray.
Do not go gentle into that good night.
Rage, rage against the dying of the light.

 Dylan Thomas

Death, be not proud …

Death, be not proud, though some have called thee
Mighty and dreadful, for thou art not so:
For those whom thou think'st thou dost overthrow
Die not, poor Death; nor yet canst thou kill me.
5   From Rest and Sleep, which but thy pictures be,
Much pleasure, then from thee much more must flow;
And soonest our best men with thee do go –
Rest of their bones and souls' delivery!
Thou'rt slave to fate, chance, kings, and desperate men,
10   And dost with poison, war, and sickness dwell;
And poppy or charms can make us sleep as well
And better than thy stroke. Why swell'st thou then?
     One short sleep past, we wake eternally,
     And death shall be no more: Death, thou shalt die!

p.207   *John Donne*

Sea Canes

Half my friends are dead.
I will make you new ones, said earth.
No, give me them back as they were, instead,
with faults and all, I cried.

5   Tonight I can snatch their talk
from the faint surf's drone
through the canes, but I cannot walk

on the moonlit leaves of ocean
down that white road alone,
10   or float with the dreaming motion

of owls leaving earth's load.
O earth, the number of friends you keep
exceeds those left to be loved.

The sea canes by the cliff flash green and silver;

15   they were the seraph lances of my faith,

but out of what is lost grows something stronger

that has the rational radiance of stone,

enduring moonlight, further than despair,

strong as the wind, that through dividing canes

20   brings those we love before us, as they were,

with faults and all, not nobler, just there.

Derek Walcott

Notes and questions

Some of the poems in this section concern the death of a beloved relative, or the effect of such death on the persona; in others death is an occasion to discuss or reflect on life and experience; in others death itself is discussed, complained about, or mocked. Since death is final and certain, but at the same time unknown, it exerts a powerful fascination in our minds and has always been a very popular theme in literature.

 Death Came to See Me in Hot Pink Pants

- Note that the personification of 'Death' in this poem, accentuated by unusual attire, makes it very dramatic. What do you think the poem is saying about death?

- How does the poet's awakening (line 20) resolve the questions raised by the poem? What do the last two lines do to adjust our final perspective on this 'dream'?

 Mid-Term Break

- Note how this poem works by releasing information slowly throughout. It is only at the end that the reader knows what has happened. Do you find this technique effective? If so why?

- Who has died? What was his relationship to the persona? How old was he? How do you think he died?

- In what stanza do we get most of this information?

 For Fergus

Fergus Lawrence was a St Lucian intellectual and supporter of the arts who died quite young.

- The persona's attitude towards the dying Fergus is different from her attitude when he is dead. What is this difference and can you explain it?

 Piazza Piece

- There are two voices in this poem. Whose is the voice in the first stanza? Whose is the voice in the second stanza?

- To whom are the first four lines of the poem addressed?

- To whom are the last two lines of the poem addressed?

- What do the last two lines of stanza 1 mean?

- What do you think the following lines symbolise:
  - 'roses on your trellis dying' (line 5)
  - 'the spectral singing of the moon' (line 6)?

- What is the significance of the description of the man in stanza 2: 'But what grey man …/Whose words are dry and faint …' (lines 11–12)?

- Why does the lady rebuke the old man?

It Was the Singing

'long-metre' (line 4) – long-winded sermon.

- Note how, by mentioning several people by name, the poet suggests a tight-knit community in mourning for one of its own, and how the daily problems, as well as the sorrow, are transcended through the singing at the funeral: 'It was then I know we was people/together' (lines 19–20).

Sylvester's Dying Bed

- In what way do the tone and language of this poem affect the response of the reader? Is it a funny poem?

- Does Sylvester accept that he is dying, or does he want to keep on living? Or are both of these true?

- Does Sylvester seem to be a likeable character? If so why?

Old Age Gets Up

- Compare this poem with 'Death Came to See Me in Hot Pink Pants'. Note that both poems make use of the device of personification and both involve references to apparel.

- What other techniques are used in this poem to make 'old age' more vivid and memorable?

Because I Could Not Stop for Death

'Gossamer' (line 15) – a light transparent fabric.

'Tippet' (line 16) – a type of scarf or cape worn over or around the neck or shoulders.

'Tulle' (line 16) – a fine net-like fabric used for veils, hats, etc.

'Swelling of the Ground' (line 18) – refers to the grave in which the dead persona is buried.

- Again, in this poem death is personified. Note that the poet, Emily Dickinson, faces the challenge of making the reader aware of what is going on, while keeping the persona only partly aware. This has the effect of a very powerful irony, reinforced by the matter-of-fact, conversational style.

Requiem

- Who is the poet commemorating and mourning in this poem?

- How and when did they die?

- Why does the poet feel the need to mourn them at this time?

Death

- In stanzas 1–4 the poet is making a point about light. What is this point?

- What is the common thing that happens to 'all' (line 15) at death?

- What is the distinction made between 'the jewelled skin of any fish' in death (lines 1–4) and 'the open stare of any fish in death' (lines 17–19)?

- To what does 'dappled light' (line 16) refer?

Amerindian

'Amerindian' (title) – name of the native people in Guyana, where this poem is set.

- Why does the old Amerindian look awkward and out of place?

- What is the poet saying about the values of the 'town' and those of the native people of the interior?

November

- Why is the persona deleting his contacts? What do the following lines suggest: '… those who are beyond the reach of phone calls, computer messages, letters/ and the grasping of my voice whether i howl or whisper.' (lines 3–4)?

- Comment on the progression of the weather images from 'drizzle' (line 11) to 'rain' (line 12). What do these images symbolise in the poem?

- Why do the numbers 'begin to blur' (line 16)?

- What do you infer from the persona's reaction in the last two lines of the poem?

An Abandoned Bundle

'White City Jabavu' (line 3) – an urban area near Soweto and Johannesburg in South Africa.

- Explain how the words and images in stanza 1 set the tone of the poem and prepare us for the revelation in stanza 4.

- What does 'Oh! Baby in the Manger' (line 19) call to mind? Why is this ironic?

- Is the poet being ironic in the last two lines of the poem?

I Heard a Fly Buzz – When I Died

Emily Dickinson has written several poems in which she imagines herself dead.

- To what familiar weather phenomenon does the poet seem to be referring in lines 3–4?

- What seems to be about to happen in stanza 2?

- In stanza 3, what activity associated with death does the buzzing fly interrupt?

- Is it the buzzing fly that brings the poem to an end in stanza 4? Give reasons for your answer.

Death of a Steel Bassman

'Conway' and 'Marchand' (line 6) – two communities in the suburbs of Castries in Saint Lucia.

'Laventille' (line 7) – a community in the outskirts of Port of Spain in Trinidad.

'sigawèt of tabak' (line 10) – A French-Creole term: 'sigawèt' is a cigarette and 'tabak' is tobacco, so the phrase means a tobacco cigarette.

- The poet pays tribute to the sound of the bass as played by the bassman. Point out the lines that describe the qualities of the sound appreciated by the speaker.

- What is the 'it' referred to in the last line of the poem?

- Find and explain the similes in the poem.

Dead Boy

- What do you think the following refer to in this poem:

    - 'Virginia's aged tree' (line 2)

    - '… kinned by poor pretense/With a noble house' (lines 10–11)

    - '… the forbears' antique lineaments' (line 12)

    - '… a deep dynastic wound' (line 16)?

- To whom does 'a green bough' refer in line 2?

- What is the relationship of the 'little cousin' to the others mentioned in the poem?

- Explain the meaning of line 19: 'But this was the old tree's late branch wrenched away,'

- What are the reactions to the death of the 'little cousin'?

p.199 *Tropical Death*
- What are the elements of a 'tropical death'?

- What are some ways in which it differs from death in some 'North Europe' countries? Find the lines that explicitly state a difference and those that imply a difference, and state what these differences are.

p.200 *Do Not Go Gentle into That Good Night*
- What is the 'good night' referred to in the poem? Why is the poet against the gentle acceptance of it?

- In the last stanza it becomes clear that the person really being addressed in the poem is the poet's father. What do the poet's own feelings have to do with his call for 'rage' against death?

p.201 *Death, be not proud ...*
The argument in lines 5–6 is that rest and sleep are a little bit like death, and since these give us some pleasure and renewal we should expect even more from death.

In lines 9–12 the persona scoffs at the so-called 'pride' and 'power' of death – death is no better than 'poison', 'war', 'sickness' and all the other agents that kill men.

- The last two lines (13–14) indicate why the poet is not afraid of death. What is his confidence of survival based on?

p.201 *Sea Canes*
- According to stanza 4, what causes the poet's anxiety about his departed friends?

- Explain the meaning of the contrast in stanzas 5 and 6 between the 'green and silver' (line 14) flash of the sea canes and the 'rational radiance of stone' (line 17). How does the poet feel by the end of the poem?

- What are 'sea canes'? How would you explain the title of this poem?

Reading and enjoying poetry

Many students around CSEC age seem to be afraid of poems. They try to avoid them as much as possible, and when they can't, they approach them with dread, expecting the worst. It is true that for years the mean marks for the poetry questions on the CSEC paper have been among the lowest. This is a sad situation when one considers that poems exist mainly to give pleasure – as is the case with most creative writing. Poems are to be read aloud and enjoyed rather than approached as a difficult puzzle to be solved. Poems are in fact the most natural form of literary expression, the closest to ordinary speech and the first literary form that you encounter, long before you start going to school. The nursery rhymes, songs and jingles that you learned and enjoyed as very young children were poems – you can tell from looking at them. You can recognise a poem on the page because it consists of a string of individual lines, rather than paragraphs or solid blocks of writing. The lines can be long, marching or galloping right across the page, or short, descending swiftly down the middle like a narrow staircase. You can see how the very appearance of a poem can suggest movement or impart a feeling about it, even before the words are read. Whatever the appearance of poems on the page, however, they all share the same basic unit, the line, unlike prose where the unit is the sentence or paragraph.

Because a poem is built of lines of words and is really meant to be read aloud, it has a special quality of sound which builds into a recognisable pattern that we call *rhythm*. All poems have rhythm, which consists of repeated patterns of stressed and unstressed syllables. Poems are like music, and in earlier times many were sung and accompanied by instruments such as the lute. So poems have a *beat*, like music, and the word 'rhythm' can be used to talk about both music and poetry. Note how the stressed (underlined) syllables determine the particular beat in the opening lines of 'The Lady's-Maid's Song' (p.99):

When <u>Ad</u>am <u>found</u> his <u>rib</u> was <u>gone</u>

He <u>cursed</u> and <u>sighed</u> and <u>cried</u> and <u>swore</u>,

And <u>looked</u> with <u>cold</u> re<u>sent</u>ment <u>on</u>

The <u>creat</u>ure <u>God</u> had <u>used</u> it <u>for</u>.

Here you get a regular pattern of an unstressed syllable followed by a stressed syllable. This is known as *iambic metre*. It is the most common metre in English poetry and is closest to the rhythm of ordinary speech in English language. There is no need for you to learn all the technical terms for the various metres at this stage, though you should be aware that there are several and they all produce different effects. What you need to notice as you read a poem aloud is the pace of the rhythm, whether quick or slow, and its appropriateness to the subject or *mood* of the poem. The rhythm can help you to understand a poem, as it is an important part of a poem's meaning. Always remember that in talking about a poem it is never any use simply to draw attention to the pattern of stresses nor just to mention the technical terms for the various sound patterns; you must show that these have some relationship to the poem's meaning. If you can't relate a rhythmic effect that you notice to the poem's meaning, it is better not to say anything about it.

Another important sound device found in many poems is *rhyme*, when words at the ends of different lines have the same sound, as in these lines from 'Aunt Jennifer's Tigers' (p.39):

Aunt Jennifer's tigers prance across a <u>screen</u>,

Bright topaz denizens of a world of <u>green</u>.

There is also *internal rhyme*, when a sound in the middle of a line is repeated at the end, but this should only be mentioned if it draws attention to something important or creates a special effect to emphasise some aspect of the poem's meaning. Sometimes rhymes occur in a regular pattern throughout the poem and the poem is said to have a *rhyme scheme*. In some poems the rhymes do not form a pattern and the poem is said to have *irregular rhyme*; in others the rhymes only occur in a few places, and this is called *occasional rhyme*.

There are other sound devices you should know about, such as *assonance* and *alliteration* (see the 'Glossary of terms'), and these all help to indicate the importance of sound to poetry. It is important to stress, therefore, the need to experience a poem's sound patterns by reading it aloud before attempting to write about it.

After you have noticed its physical appearance on the page and noted its sound patterns, you have to deal with the language of the poem – the words and what they mean. We use the word *diction* to refer to the way words are used in a poem; not single words, usually, but the general quality of the words used. We speak of a poem's diction as being 'concrete' (where the words refer predominantly to real things), 'abstract' (where they refer mainly to ideas and imprecise feelings), 'colloquial' or 'formal', 'technical' or 'common', and so on. Another thing to remember about words in poems is that they don't only mean what the dictionary says they mean (*denote*). They can also conjure up in your mind other words and associations, feelings and scraps of memory (particularly of other places and poems where you have encountered the same word in the past), ideas and experiences. This property of words in a poem is known as their ability to *connote* and the *connotative* meaning of a word is often more important in a poem than its *denotative* meaning. In this way poems, even very brief ones, expand ever outward and seem to become larger works with richer meanings and deeper feelings than appeared possible when you first saw them on the page.

Of course words are also woven into *images* and other *figures of speech*, which are very important in poetry. These paint pictures and appeal to all of our senses. Look at how the poet (Yeats, in this case) makes us see, hear and feel certain things in the following lines from 'Sailing to Byzantium' (p.181):

An aged man is but a paltry thing,

A tattered coat upon a stick, unless

Soul clap its hands and sing, and louder sing

For every tatter in its mortal dress,

Nor is there singing school but studying

Monuments of its own magnificence;

As we read these lines the *imagery* helps us to understand it by recreating for us something of the experience of the feeling which prompted the poet to write the poem. Such communication of feeling and experience (and the pleasure to be had from it) is the main purpose of poetry. Types of image and specific figures of speech have names you should learn like *simile*, *metaphor*, *personification*, and so on (see the 'Glossary of terms').

Words, images and the other components of a poem work together to create the less concrete attributes that you also have to be aware of and discuss when you answer questions on poetry. For example, there is an overall feeling projected by a poem which in some cases builds powerfully to the point where it predominates and claims almost all our attention. This is called the *mood* or *atmosphere* of the poem. Some poems are written simply to create atmosphere or to evoke a particular mood, but in most poems it is possible to identify a mood or several moods as the poem progresses. Look, for example, at the mood created in the last seven lines of the poem 'Ethics' (p.172):

… The colors

within this frame are darker than autumn,

darker even than winter – the browns of earth,

though earth's most radiant elements burn

through the canvas. I know now that woman

and painting and season are almost one

and all beyond the saving of children.

Here the words and images create a dark or sombre mood stressing the burdens of old age and the power of great art – and this contrasts utterly with the earlier childish concerns depicted in the poem: the questions about art and age and life become more serious and urgent as the persona recognises that these are beyond the shallow understanding of many school children. Students sometimes confuse the mood of a poem with its *tone*. Tone is associated with the tone of voice, and therefore the attitude of the poet towards the subject of his poem. The tone can be 'detached', 'sympathetic', 'sarcastic', 'quarrelsome', and so on, whereas mood, as we have seen, is the predominant feeling created by the poem.

There are, of course, many types of poems. There are *narrative poems*, where the principal function is to tell a story and *descriptive poems*, which communicate ideas and feelings about people, objects and landscapes by describing selected details. There are *mood poems*, as described above, which also fall into the category called *lyrical poems*, which are usually written in the first person and express a state of mind or a process of thought or feeling. *Epic poems* are long narrative poems which are associated with the history or identity of a people. *Elegies*, or *elegiac poems*, mourn the dead or look back with regret at something which no longer exists. There are also many terms for the various forms of poems (e.g. the sonnet form), but there is no need to learn all of these. Your teacher will tell you, as you study a particular poem, what category it belongs to; you can also check the notes on the poems at the end of each section.

These are some of the basic things you need to know about poems and how they communicate meaning. As with all things, detailed knowledge dispels fear! The more you read poetry and the more you practise trying to talk about it in the terms outlined here (and those taught in class), the less you will be afraid of poems. There is a world of enjoyment in a collection of poetry and your first attitude towards this one should be a desire to experience the pleasure of reading the poems – technical understanding will come afterwards.

Checklist for reading a poem

1 Subject matter

- Who is speaking? (speaker)
- In what situation? (occasion)
- To whom? (addressee)
- Privately or publicly?
- About what? (subject or theme)
- What is said? (thesis)
- Directly or indirectly?
- What common human concerns does this touch on? (universality)

2 Sound

- What does the sound pattern tell you?
- Is the rhythm quick or slow?
- Does the rhythm suit/reinforce the subject matter?
- Is there rhyme?
- Does the rhyme contribute to your understanding/enjoyment of the poem?
- Is there any interesting or appropriate use of alliteration/assonance?

3 Diction

- Are the words simple or complicated?
- Sophisticated or naive?
- Formal or conversational?
- Smooth or rough?
- Many-syllabled or monosyllabic?
- How does the diction contribute to the meaning/mood?

4 Imagery

- Is the imagery striking or ordinary?
- Easily understood or obscure?

- Is the principal appeal to the sense of sight or hearing, touch, etc?
- Is the imagery functional or ornamental?
- Is the imagery symbolic?
- Is the symbolism natural, conventional or original?

5 Mood and tone

- How would you describe the mood of the poem?
- Is the poem more thoughtful than emotional?
- More emotional than thoughtful?
- Are thought and emotion balanced in the poem?
- Is the tone of the poem serious or light?
- Is it ironical, satirical, sentimental, sincere, flippant, etc?

6 Organic consistency

- Do all the items above fuse into an organic whole?
- Are there any elements (imagery, diction, etc.) which appear unsuited to the rest of the poem?
- Are there any elements which don't seem to have a good reason for being there?

7 Do you like the poem? If you were putting together an anthology of good poems, would you include the poem? For what particular reasons?

Glossary of terms

alliteration a sound effect caused by the repetition of stressed consonant sounds

assonance a sound effect consisting of the repetition of stressed vowel sounds

blank verse unrhymed five-stress lines, principally of iambic metre (iambic pentameters); Milton's *Paradise Lost* and most of Shakespeare's plays are written in blank verse

caesura a pause in a line of poetry, usually dependent on the sense of the line and indicated by a strong punctuation mark

connotation the secondary meanings and associations suggested to the reader by a particular word or phrase, as opposed to denotation or dictionary meaning

couplet two lines of the same metre which rhyme

denotation the meaning of a word according to the dictionary, as opposed to its connotations

elegy a formal poem lamenting the death of a particular person

epic a long narrative poem, usually celebrating some aspect of the history or identity of a people; Dante's *Divine Comedy* and Milton's *Paradise Lost* are examples of epic poems

epic simile a simile extending over several lines, in which the object of comparison is described at great length

eye rhyme a pair of syllables which appear to the eye as though they should rhyme, but which do not, such as 'have' and 'wave'

figurative language non-literal expressions used to convey more vividly certain ideas and feelings; includes such figures as simile, metaphor and personification

form either the appearance of poetry on the page or a way of referring to the structure of the poem – its division into stanzas, etc.

free verse poetry that has no regular rhythmic pattern (metre)

hyperbole a type of figurative language consisting of exaggeration or overstatement

imagery vivid description of an object or a scene; the term is also applied to figurative language, particularly to examples of simile and metaphor

irony a device whereby the apparent meaning of a phrase or passage is different from the meaning it is really intended to convey

lyric a type of poetry that is a personal statement evoking a mood or expressing a certain feeling

metaphor a type of figurative language in which one thing is described in a way that identifies it with something else

metre the regular pattern of stressed and unstressed syllables that we hear over several lines of poetry

mood the dominant feeling evoked by the words, images and other devices used in a poem

onomatopoeia a word or group of words whose sound suggests its meaning, such as 'hiss' or 'murmur'

pastoral a highly conventional poetic form which celebrates the world of shepherds and other country people

personification when a poet refers to an inanimate object or an abstract quality as though it were a living person

quatrain a four-line stanza or group of lines, usually rhyming

rhyme the repetition of the last stressed vowel sound in a word together with any unstressed sounds that follow, as in <u>gate</u>, <u>late</u>, and <u>cover</u>, <u>lover</u>; there are special terms that describe different kinds of rhyme (see notes in 'Reading and enjoying poetry')

rhyme scheme the pattern of rhymed endings of lines within a stanza or short poem; the first rhymed sounds can be labelled a, the second b, and so on

rhythm the recurrence of groups of stressed and unstressed syllables in lines of poetry (see notes in 'Reading and enjoying poetry')

run-on lines lines in which the meaning leads you to run swiftly beyond the end of the line and into the next line to complete the syntax and the sense, as in these lines from 'Ol' Higue' (p.159):

> You think I wouldn't rather
>
> take my blood seasoned in fat
>
> black-pudding, like everyone else?

simile a figure of speech in which an explicit comparison is made between two things, using 'like', 'as' or 'than'

sonnet a form of poem almost always consisting of 14 five-stressed lines; the two main types of sonnet are the English or Shakespearean sonnet (distinguished by its final couplet), and the Italian or Petrarchan sonnet, consisting of a group of eight lines (the *octave)* followed by a group of six lines (the *sestet)*

stanza a group of lines forming one of the divisions of a poem

stress refers to the prominence or emphasis given to certain words or syllables when they are spoken; stress is a prominent feature of English speech and therefore of the rhythm of poetry in English

synecdoche a figure of speech in which a part is used for a whole, an individual for a class, or the reverse of these, for example, '$5 per head' means '$5 per person'

tercet a three-line stanza or a group of three lines within a stanza or a poem

tone the poet's attitude or tone of voice; the tone gives a clue as to how the poem is to be read, or reinforces other aspects of the poem's meaning (see notes in 'Reading and enjoying poetry')

Acknowledgements

Every effort has been made to trace all copyright holders, but if any have been inadvertently overlooked the Publishers will be pleased to make the necessary arrangements at the first opportunity. The Publishers would like to thank the following for permission to reproduce copyright material:

p.2 'Childhood of a Voice' by Martin Carter from SELECTED POEMS, published by Peepal Tree Press. Reprinted by permission of the publishers; **p.2** 'A Lesson for this Sunday' by Derek Walcott from COLLECTED POEMS 1948–1984, published by Faber and Faber Limited. Reprinted by permission of the publishers (audio reproduced by permission of Farrar, Straus and Giroux); **p.3** 'Hurt Hawks' copyright © 1928 and renewed 1956 by Robinson Jeffers; from THE SELECTED POETRY OF ROBINSON JEFFERS by Robinson Jeffers. Used by permission of Random House, an imprint and division of Penguin Random House LLC. All rights reserved (audio reproduced by permission of Stanford University Press); **p.4** 'Birdshooting Season' by Olive Senior from TALKING OF TREES. Reprinted with the kind permission of the author; **p.5** 'Hedgehog' by Paul Muldoon from POEMS 1968–1998, published by Faber and Faber Limited. Reprinted by permission of the publishers; **p.6** 'Schooldays' by Stanley Greaves from HORIZONS, published by Peepal Tree Press. Reprinted by permission of the publishers; **p.7** 'An African Thunderstorm' from AN AFRICAN THUNDERSTORM AND OTHER POEMS by David Rubardiri, published by East African Educational Publishers. Reprinted with permission of the publishers; **p.8** 'Those Winter Sundays' copyright © 1966 by Robert Hayden, from COLLECTED POEMS OF ROBERT HAYDEN by Robert Hayden, edited by Frederick Glaysher. Used by permission of Liveright Publishing Corporation; **p.8** 'A Quartet of Daffodils' by Lorna Goodison from TURN, THANKS: POEMS. Copyright 1999 by Lorna Goodison. Used with permission of the University of Illinois Press; **p.10** 'Landscape Painter, Jamaica' by Vivian Virtue from WINGS OF THE EVENING: SELECTED POEMS OF VIVIAN VIRTUE, published by Ian Randle Publishers; **p.11** 'Janet Waking' by John Crowe Ransom, from SELECTED POEMS, published by Carcanet Press Limited 1991. Reprinted by permission of the publishers; **p.12** 'Their Lonely Betters' by W.H. Auden from NONES, published by Faber & Faber Limited, 1951; **p.12** 'Responsibility' by Edward Baugh which first appeared in IT WAS THE SINGING, published by Sandberry Press in 2000 © Edward Baugh 2000; **p.13** 'Dove Song' by Esther Phillips, from WHEN GROUND DOVES FLY, published by Ian Randle Publishers, 2003. Reprinted with the kind permission of the author; **p.14** 'Ground Doves' by Lorna Goodison from TO US, ALL FLOWERS ARE ROSES: POEMS. Copyright 1995 Lorna Goodison. Used with permission of the University of Illinois Press; **p.15** 'Horses' by Mahadai Das from A LEAF IN HIS EAR, published by Peepal Tree Press. Reprinted by permission of the publishers; **p.16** 'Keep off the Grass' by Oswald Mbuyiseni Mtshali, from SOUNDS OF A COWHIDE DRUM. Publisher: Renoster, Johannesburg, 1971. By Permission of DALRO (Pty) Ltd on behalf Oswald Mtshali;

p.22 'My Parents' by Stephen Spender from COLLECTED POEMS 1928–1985, published by Faber & Faber © 2004. Reprinted by kind permission of the Estate of Stephen Spender; **p.22** 'Journal' by David Wllliams © David Williams; **p.24** 'A Song in the Front Yard' by Gwendolyn Brooks. © Gwendolyn Brooks. Reprinted by consent of Brooks Permissions; **p.24** 'Fern Hill' by Dylan Thomas from POEMS OF DYLAN THOMAS, published by New Directions Pub. Corp., 1971. Reprinted with the kind permission of David Higham Associates/The Estate of Dylan Thomas; **p.26** 'Counter' by Merle Collins, from LADY IN A BOAT, published by Peepal Tree Press. Reprinted by permission of the publishers; **p.27** 'Overseer: Detention' by Vladimir Lucien, from SOUNDING GROUND, published by Peepal Tree Press 2014. Reprinted by permission of the publishers; **p.28** 'English Girl Eats Her First Mango' by John Agard from ALTERNATIVE ANTHEM: SELECTED POEMS (Bloodaxe Books, 2009). Reprinted with permission of Bloodaxe Books, on behalf of the author. www.bloodaxebooks.com; **p.31** 'Walking on Lily Leaves' by Ian McDonald from JAFFO THE CALYPSONIAN, published by Peepal Tree Press 1994. Reprinted by permission of the publishers; **p.32** 'Little Boy Crying' by Mervyn Morris from I BEEN THERE, SORT OF: NEW AND SELECTED POEMS, published by Carcanet Press Limited 2006. Reprinted by permission of the publishers; **p.33** 'School Play' by Hazel Simmons-McDonald from SILK COTTON AND OTHER TREES, published by Ian Randle Press, 2004. Copyright © Hazel Simmons-McDonald. Reprinted with the kind permission of the author; **p.34** 'The Child Ran Into the Sea' from MACMILLAN CARIBBEAN WRITERS: POEMS BY MARTIN CARTER. Text (poems) © Phyllis Carter 2006, published by Macmillan Publishers Limited. Used by Permission. All Rights Reserved; **p.34** 'Wharf Story' by Anthony Kellman, from LONG GAP, published by Peepal Tree Press. Reprinted by permission of the publishers; **p.35** 'Once Upon a Time' by Gabriel Okara, from THE FISHERMAN'S INVOCATION, published by Heinemann Educational Books, 1978; **p.37** 'How Dreams Grow Fat and Die' by Tanya Shirley from THE MERCHANT OF FEATHERS, published by Peepal Tree Press 2015. Reprinted by permission of the publishers; **p.38** 'Abra-Cadabra' by Grace Nichols, from THE NEW POETRY (Bloodaxe Books, 1993). Reprinted with permission of Bloodaxe Books, on behalf of the author. www.bloodaxebooks.com; **p.39** 'Aunt Jennifer's Tigers' copyright © 2016 by The Adrienne Rich Literary Trust. Copyright © 1951 by Adrienne Rich, from COLLECTED POEMS: 1950–2012 by Adrienne Rich. Used by permission of W.W. Norton & Company, Inc.; **p.39** 'Kanaima/Tiger' by Mark McWatt from THE JOURNEY TO LE REPENTIR, published by Peepal Tree Press, 2009. Copyright © Mark McWatt. Reprinted with the kind permission of the author; **p.41** 'Jamaica Journal' by Cecil Gray. Reprinted with the kind permission of the author; **p.41** 'Comfort' by Hazel Simmons-McDonald from SILK COTTON AND OTHER TREES, published by Ian Randle Press, 2004. Copyright © Hazel Simmons-McDonald. Reprinted with the kind permission of the author; **p.43** 'Boy with Book of Knowledge' by Howard Nemerov from THE COLLECTED POEMS OF HOWARD NEMEROV, The University of Chicago Press, 1977; **p.50** 'West Indies, U.S.A.' by Stewart Brown, from LUGARD'S BRIDGE, published by Seren Books 1989. Reprinted with the kind permission of Seren Books and Stewart Brown; **p.51** 'Melbourne' by Chris Wallace-Crabbe, from NEW AND SELECTED POEMS, published by Carcanet Press Limited 2013. Reprinted by permission of the publishers; **p.52** 'A Place' by Kendel Hippolyte from FAULT LINES, published by Peepal Tree Press 2012. Reprinted by permission of the publishers; **p.52** 'A View of Dingle Bay, Ireland' by Ralph Thompson from MOVING ON, published by Peepal Tree Press. Reprinted by permission of the publishers; **p.53** 'Bristol' by Kwame Dawes from NEW AND SELECTED POEMS, published by Peepal Tree Press. Reprinted by permission of the publishers; **p.55** 'On the Brooklyn Bridge' by Winston Farrell, published by Caribbean Chapters Publishing Inc. Reprinted with the kind permission of the author; **p.56** 'Castries' by Kendel Hippolyte from BIRTHRIGHT, published by Peepal Tree Press. Reprinted by permission of the publishers; **p.58** 'The Only Thing Far Away' by Kei Miller from THERE IS AN ANGER THAT MOVES, published by Carcanet 2007. Reprinted by permission of the publishers; **p.58** 'Return' by Dionne Brand. Copyright © Dionne Brand, 1998, used by permission of The Wylie Agency (UK) Limited; **p.66** 'Liminal' by Kendel Hippolyte from BIRTHRIGHT, published by Peepal Tree Press. Reprinted by permission of the publishers; **p.67** 'Swimming Chenango Lake' by Charles Tomlinson from NEW COLLECTED POEMS, published by Carcanet 2009. Reprinted by permission of the publishers; **p.68** 'A Grandfather Sings' by Jennifer Rahim, from BETWEEN THE FOREST AND THE TREES, published by Peepal Tree Press. Reprinted by permission of the publishers; **p.69** 'Basil' by Vladimir Lucien, from SOUNDING GROUND, published by Peepal Tree Press. Reprinted by permission of the publishers; **p.70** 'Cold As Heaven' by Judith Ortiz Cofer, from REACHING FOR THE MAINLAND, published by Bilingual Review Press © The Estate of Judith Ortiz Cofer. Reprinted with permission of Bilingual Review Press; **p.71** 'Dennis Street: Daddy' by Sasenarine Persaud from LOVE IN A TIME OF TECHNOLOGY, published by Peepal Tree Press. Reprinted with the kind permission of the author; **p.72** 'Hinckson' by Anthony Kellman, from LONG GAP, published by Peepal Tree Press. Reprinted by permission of the publishers; **p.73** 'The Deportee' by Stanley Niamatali from THE HINTERLANDS, published by Caribbean Press; **p.74** 'Silk Cotton Trees' by Hazel Simmons-McDonald. Copyright © Hazel Simmons-McDonald. Reprinted with the kind permission of the author; **p.75** 'Lala: The Dressmaker' by Honor Ford-Smith from MY MOTHER'S LAST DANCE, published by Sistervision Press. Reprinted with the kind permission of the author; **p.77** 'Fellow Traveller' by Jane King, which first appeared in FELLOW TRAVELLER, published by Sandberry Press, 1994. © Jane King 1994, used by permission of the poet, Jane King and Sandberry Press; **p.78** 'Drought' by Wayne Brown from ON THE COAST, published by Andre Deutsch, London 1973. © Wayne Brown 1973. Reprinted with the kind permission of the estate of Wayne Brown; **p.79** 'I Knew a Woman' by Theodore Roethke from COLLECTED POEMS, published by Faber and Faber Limited. Reprinted by permission of the publishers (ebook and audio reproduced by permission of Doubleday, an imprint of the Knopf Doubleday Publishing Group, a division of Penguin Random House LLC. All rights reserved); **p.80** 'Betrothal' by Ian McDonald from BETWEEN SILENCE AND SILENCE, published by Peepal Tree Press. Reprinted by permission of the publishers; **p.83** 'Orchids' by Hazel Simmons-McDonald. Copyright © Hazel Simmons-McDonald. Reprinted with the kind permission of the author; **p.84** 'My Grandmother' by Elizabeth Jennings from THE COLLECTED POEMS, published by Carcanet. Reprinted with the kind permission of David Higham Associates/The Estate of Elizabeth Jennings; **p.85** 'The Zulu Girl' from ADAMASTOR by Roy Campbell. By Permission of DALRO (Pty) Ltd on behalf of Roy Campbell Estate; **p.85** 'The Woman Speaks to the Man who has Employed her Son' by Lorna Goodison, from GUINEA WOMAN, published by Carcanet Press Limited 2000. Reprinted by permission of the publishers; **p.87** 'Elegy for Jane' by Theodore Roethke from COLLECTED POEMS, published by Faber and Faber Limited. Reprinted by permission of the publishers (ebook and audio reproduced by permission of Doubleday, an imprint of the Knopf Doubleday Publishing Group, a division of Penguin Random House LLC. All rights reserved); **p.88** 'Apartment Neighbours' by Velma Pollard, from SHAME TREES DON'T GROW HERE, published by Peepal Tree Press. Reprinted by permission of the publishers; **p.89** 'Koo' by Kendel Hippolyte, from BIRTHRIGHT, published by Peepal Tree Press. Reprinted by permission of the publishers; **p.90** 'Abraham and Isaac After' by Lorna Goodison, from GOLDEN GROVE: NEW AND SELECTED POEMS, published by Carcanet 2006. Reprinted by permission of the publishers; **p.99** 'Come Breakfast with Me' by Mahadai Das, from A LEAF IN HIS EAR: COLLECTED POEMS, published by Peepal Tree Press. Reprinted by permission of the publishers; **p.99** 'The Lady's-Maid's Song' from SELECTED POETRY by John Hollander, copyright © 1993 by John Hollander. Used by permission of Alfred A. Knopf, an imprint of the Knopf Doubleday Publishing Group, a division of Penguin Random House LLC. All rights reserved (audio rights © the Hollander Trust); **p.100** 'Koraibo' by Mark McWatt. Copyright © Mark McWatt. Reprinted with the kind permission of the author; **p.102** 'Nexus' by Esther Phillips from THE STONE GATHERERS, published by Peepal Tree Press. Reprinted by permission of the publishers; **p.103** 'Close to You Now' by Lorna Goodison, from TURN, THANKS: POEMS. Copyright 1999 by Lorna Goodison. Used with permission of the University of Illinois Press; **p.104** 'Lullaby' by W. H. Auden, from COLLECTED POEMS, published by Faber & Faber Limited, 2004; **p.105** 'Hate' by David Eva, from SUNBURST edited by Ian Gordon, published by Heinemann; **p.107** 'It is the Constant Image of Your Face' by Dennis Brutus from A SIMPLE LUST, published by Heinemann, 1973; **p.112** 'The Last Sign of the Cross' by Vladimir Lucien from SOUNDING GROUND, published by Peepal Tree Press. Reprinted by permission of the publishers; **p.113** 'Jesus is Nailed to the Cross' from DE MAN: A PERFORMANCE POEM is used by permission of the author, Pamela Mordecai; **p.114** 'A Stone's Throw' by Elma Mitchell, from PEOPLE ETCETERA: POEMS NEW AND SELECTED, published by Peterloo Poets; **p.116** 'Burnt Offerings' by Hazel Simmons-McDonald. Copyright © Hazel Simmons-McDonald. Reprinted with the kind permission of the author; **p.118** 'The Convert's Defence' by Stanley Niamatali from THE HINTERLANDS, published by Caribbean Press; **p.124** 'Test Match Sabina Park' by Stewart Brown, from ZINDER published by Poetry Wales Press 1986. Reprinted with the kind permission of Seren Books and Stewart Brown; **p.125** 'Theme for English B' by Langston Hughes, from THE COLLECTED POEMS OF LANGSTON HUGHES, published by Alfred A. Knopf Inc. Reprinted with the kind permission of David Higham Associates/The Estate of Langston Hughes; **p.126** 'Vendor' by Esther Phillips from THE STONE GATHERERS, published by Peepal Tree Press. Reprinted by permission of the publishers; **p.127** 'Dinner Guest: Me' by Langston Hughes from NEGRO DIGEST 1965. Reprinted with the kind permission of David Higham Associates/The Estate of Langston Hughes; **p.128** 'Dreaming Black Boy' from WHEN I DANCE by James Berry reprinted by permission of Peters Fraser & Dunlop (www.petersfraserdunlop.com) on behalf of James Berry; **p.129** 'Caribbean History' by Stanley Greaves, from HORIZONS, published by Peepal Tree Press. Reprinted by permission of the publishers; **p.130** 'Black' by Dennis Craig from NEAR THE SEASHORE: COLLECTED POEMS, published by Education & Development Services, 1996. Reprinted with the kind permission of Zellynne Jennings Craig; **p.131** 'The House Slave' copyright © 1989 by Rita Dove, from COLLECTED POEMS: 1974–2004 by Rita Dove. Used by permission of W.W. Norton & Company, Inc.; **p.131** 'Attention' by Mildelense from POEMS OF BLACK AFRICA edited by Wole Soyinka, published by Heinemann Educational Books, 1975; **p.132** 'The Sleeping Zemis' by Lorna Goodison, from GUINEA WOMAN, published by Carcanet Press Limited 2000. Reprinted with permission of the publishers; **p.133** 'Booker T. and W.E.B.' from ROSES AND REVOLUTIONS: THE SELECTED WRITINGS OF DUDLEY RANDALL (Detroit: Wayne State University Press, 2010). Reprinted by permission of the Dudley Randall Literary Estate; **p.135** 'There's a Brown Girl in the Ring' by Eddie Baugh, which first appeared in IT WAS THE SINGING, published by Sandberry Press in 2000 © Edward Baugh 2000. Used by permission of the poet, Edward Baugh and Sandberry Press; **p.136** 'Whales' by Stewart Brown, from ELSEWHERE, published by Peepal Tree Press. Reprinted by permission of the publishers; **p.137** 'Goodman's Bay II' by Christian Campbell from RUNNING THE DUSK, published by Peepal Tree Press. Reprinted by permission of the publishers; **p.142** 'Listening to Sirens' by Tony Harrison, published by Faber and Faber Limited. Reprinted by permission of the publishers; **p.143** 'This is the dark time, my love' from MACMILLAN CARIBBEAN WRITERS: POEMS BY MARTIN CARTER. Text (poems) © Phyllis Carter 2006, published by Macmillan Publishers Limited. Used by Permission. All Rights Reserved; **p.144** 'Other People' by Chris Wallace-Crabbe, from NEW AND SELECTED POEMS, published by Carcanet Press Limited 2013. Reprinted by permission of the publishers; **p.145** 'War' by Joseph Langland, in JOSEPH LANGLAND SELECTED POEMS. Copyright © 1991 by Joseph Langland and published by the University of Massachusetts Press; **p.146** 'Poem' by Jorge Rebelo from POEMS OF BLACK AFRICA edited by Wole Soyinka, published by Heinemann Educational Books, 1975; **p.148** 'Song of War' by Kofi Awoonor, from NIGHT OF MY BLOOD (Garden City NY: Doubleday Anchor, 1971). Reprinted with the kind permission of Sika Awoonor; **p.153** 'The Visit' by Wayne Brown from ON THE COAST, published by Andre Deutsch, London 1973. © Wayne Brown 1973. Reprinted with the kind permission of the estate of Wayne Brown; **p.154** 'Tjenbwa: Night

Shift' by Vladimir Lucien from SOUNDING GROUND, published by Peepal Tree Press. Reprinted by permission of the publishers; **p.154** 'My Mother's Sea Chanty' by Lorna Goodison, from GUINEA WOMAN, published by Carcanet Press Limited 2000. Reprinted with permission of the publishers; **p.155** 'Mirror' by Sylvia Plath from COLLECTED POEMS, published by Faber and Faber Limited. Reprinted by permission of the publishers; **p.156** 'A Bat at Dusk' by Mark McWatt from THE JOURNEY TO LE REPENTIR, published by Peepal Tree Press, 2009. Copyright © Mark McWatt. Reprinted with the kind permission of the author; **p.158** 'Encounter' by Mervyn Morris from I BEEN THERE, SORT OF: NEW AND SELECTED POEMS, published by Carcanet Press Limited 2006. Reprinted by permission of the publishers; **p.159** 'Ol' Higue' by Mark McWatt from THE LANGUAGE OF EL DORADO, published by Dangaroo Press, 1994. Copyright © Mark McWatt. Reprinted with the kind permission of the author; **p.166** 'A True Poem' by Trefossa from TROTJI PUËMA, published by NV Noord-Hollandsche Uitgevers Mij, 1957; **p.166** 'Photos' by Cynthia Wilson, from THE HIBISCUS BEARS A BLUE FLOWER, published by Cynthia Wilson in 2004 © Cynthia Wilson 2004. Reprinted with the kind permission of the author; **p.167** 'Bird' by Kendel Hippolyte from FAULT LINES, published by Peepal Tree Press. Reprinted by permission of the publishers; **p.169** 'Swan and Shadow' by John Hollander, from TYPES OF SHAPE, Yale University Press 1991 © John Hollander, 1969, 1991. Used by permission of Yale University Press; **p.169** 'Sad Steps' by Philip Larkin from COLLECTED POEMS, published by Faber and Faber Limited. Reprinted by permission of the publishers; **p.170** 'Why I'm Not A Painter' by Frank O'Hara from WHY I'M NOT A PAINTER AND OTHER POEMS, published by Carcanet Press Limited 2003. Reprinted by permission of the publishers; **p.171** 'Sonnet to a Broom' by Mahadai Das, from A LEAF IN HIS EAR, published by Peepal Tree Press. Reprinted by permission of the publishers; **p.172** 'Ethics' Copyright © 1981 by Linda Pastan, from CARNIVAL EVENING: NEW AND SELECTED POEMS 1968–1998 by Linda Pastan. Used by permission of W.W. Norton & Company, Inc. (ebook reproduced by permission of Linda Pastan in care of the Jean V. Naggar Literary Agency, Inc.); **p.176** 'Himself at Last' by Slade Hopkinson, from SNOWSCAPE WITH SIGNATURE, published by Peepal Tree Press. Reprinted by permission of the publishers; **p.176** 'Return' (for Kamau Brathwaite) by Kwame Dawes, from NEW AND SELECTED POEMS, published by Peepal Tree Press. Reprinted by permission of the publishers; **p.177** 'South' by Kamau Brathwaite from THE ARRIVANTS, published by Oxford University Press, 1973. By permission of Oxford University Press; **p.179** 'When I Loved You: Four Memories' by Mark McWatt from THE LANGUAGE OF EL DORADO, published by Dangaroo Press, 1994. Copyright © Mark McWatt. Reprinted with the kind permission of the author; **p.185** 'Death Came to See Me in Hot Pink Pants' by Heather Royes, from DAYS AND NIGHTS OF THE BLUE IGUANA, published by Peepal Tree Press. Reprinted by permission of the publishers; **p.185** 'Mid-Term Break' by Seamus Heaney from DEATH OF A NATURALIST, published by Faber and Faber Limited. Reprinted by permission of the publishers; **p.186** 'For Fergus' by Jane King, which first appeared in FELLOW TRAVELLER, published by Sandberry Press, 1994. © Jane King

1994. Used by permission of the poet, Jane King and Sandberry Press; **p.187** 'Piazza Piece' by John Crowe Ransome, from SELECTED POEMS, first published by Alfred A. Knopf, 1969, published by Carcanet Press Limited 1995. Reprinted by permission of the publishers; **p.188** 'It Was the Singing' by Edward Baugh which first appeared in IT WAS THE SINGING, published by Sandberry Press in 2000 © Edward Baugh 2000. Used by permission of the poet, Edward Baugh and Sandberry Press; **p.189** 'Sylvester's Dying Bed' by Langston Hughes from SELECTED POEMS OF LANGSTON HUGHES, published by Alfred A. Knopf Inc. Reprinted with the kind permission of David Higham Associates/The Estate of Langston Hughes; **p.190** 'Old Age Gets Up' by Ted Hughes from MOORTOWN DIARY, published by Faber and Faber Limited. Reprinted by permission of the publishers; **p.192** 'Requiem' by Kwame Dawes, NEW AND SELECTED POEMS, published by Peepal Tree Press. Reprinted by permission of the publishers; **p.193** 'Death' by Jennifer Rahim from BETWEEN THE FENCE AND THE FOREST, published by Peepal Tree Press. Reprinted by permission of the publishers; **p.194** 'Amerindian' by Ian McDonald from MERCY WARD, published by Peterloo Poets, 1988. Reprinted with the kind permission of the author; **p.195** 'November' by Kendel Hippolyte, from FAULT LINES, published by Peepal Tree Press. Reprinted by permission of the publishers; **p.195** 'An Abandoned Bundle' by Oswald Mbuyiseni Mtshali, from SOUNDS OF A COWHIDE DRUM. Publisher: Renoster, Johannesburg, 1971. By Permission of DALRO (Pty) Ltd on behalf Oswald Mtshali; **p.197** 'Death of a Steel Bassman' by Vladimir Lucien, from SOUNDING GROUND, published by Peepal Tree Press. Reprinted by permission of the publishers; **p.198** 'Dead Boy' by John Crowe Ransome, first published in TWO GENTLEMEN IN BONDS, Knopf 1927. Published by Carcanet Press Limited 1995. Reprinted by permission of the publishers; **p.199** 'Tropical Death' by Grace Nichols, from THE FAT BLACK WOMAN'S POEMS (Virago, 1984). Reprinted with permission of Bloodaxe Books, on behalf of the author. www.bloodaxebooks.com; **p.200** 'Do Not Go Gentle into That Good Night' by Dylan Thomas, from IN COUNTRY SLEEP, AND OTHER POEMS, published by New Directions Books, 1952. Reprinted with the kind permission of David Higham Associates/The Estate of Dylan Thomas; **p.201** 'Sea Canes' from SEA GRAPES by Derek Walcott. Copyright © 1976 by Derek Walcott. Used by permission of Farrar, Straus and Giroux.

Index